Ray Reardon

Former World Professional Snooker Champion, Ray Reardon, believes that any amateur can reach an acceptable standard of play by applying basic ball sense, co-ordination and making an initial effort. In this, his first book, Reardon advises the beginner how to learn to pot and describes in detail the standard Snooker skills—grip, stance, bridging, striking and the use of the rest and the spider. Illustrated throughout with over 150 line drawings of tables reproducing the shots discussed in the text, *Classic Snooker* lays strong emphasis on positional play and the techniques of side, screw and stun. Safety play, snookering and escape play are thoroughly covered and there are appendices giving ball by ball analyses of two of the author's big breaks of 142 and 147.

Ray Reardon—six times World Champion—also describes his early life and introduction—at the age of eight—to a game which he insists must, above all, be fun to play. Packed with the sort of sound practical advice that only constant play at championship level can provide, *Classic Snooker* represents not only a coaching course for players of differing standards but also an entertaining and intelligent approach to this increasingly popular sport.

Classic Snooker

RAY REARDON

David & Charles
Newton Abbot · London · North Pomfret (VT)

British Library Cataloguing in Publication Data

Reardon, Ray
    Classic snooker.
    1. Snooker
    I. Title
    794.7'3   GV900.S6

   ISBN 0–7153–7244–0

First published 1976
Second impression 1977
Third impression 1978
Fourth impression 1979
Fifth impression 1979
Sixth impression 1982
Seventh impression 1983
Eighth impression 1984

Printed in Great Britain
by Redwood Burn Limited
Trowbridge, Wiltshire
for David & Charles (Publishers) Limited
Brunel House   Newton Abbot   Devon

Published in the United States of America
by David & Charles Inc
North Pomfret   Vermont 05053   USA

Contents

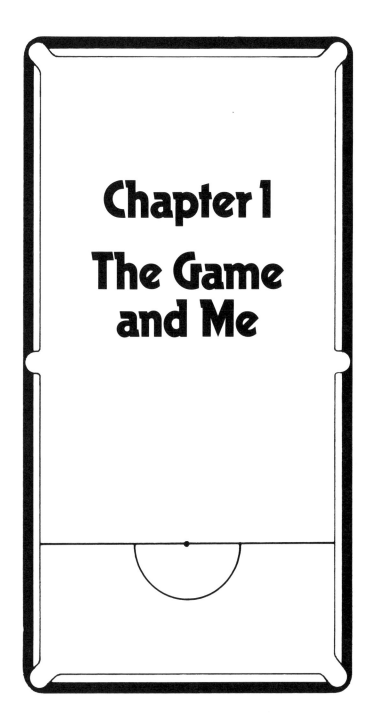

Chapter 1

The Game and Me

My father, Ben, and his four brothers were all good Snooker players and made a pretty useful team. We had a miniature table at home in Tredegar, South Wales, on which I started to play when I was about eight, so I have been playing Snooker almost as long as I can remember. At first, Uncle Dan, used to play with me at home every Sunday afternoon and then, when I was eleven or twelve, father used to take me to the local Institute on Thursday evenings, which was usually one of the less busy nights of the week. If, when I was playing, all the tables became occupied, I had to stop.

I wasn't very big and, on full-sized tables, there were lots of shots I couldn't reach. My father had played too much local competitive Snooker to stand any nonsense like climbing on the table so I quickly learned how to use the rest. By getting used to it in this way, so early in my career, I've never been afraid to employ it and, unlike some players who are otherwise very good professionals, I never try to avoid using it by overstretching or selecting another shot.

As a lad, I swam and played Cricket and Rugby but Snooker was always my game. Six of us would play Pool at sixpence a pool. I had two shillings (10p) pocket money each week: bus fare, three lost games and that was it—I was skint for a week.

While all this was happening I was extending my knowledge of angles, particularly from Skittle Pool, and playing in championships such as the Welsh Boys and British Boys (under 16), neither of which I ever won for the simple reason that I wasn't good enough. My best chance of winning anything came when I moved up to the British Youths (for under nineteen-year-olds) but I lost in the final in my last year to Jack Carney from Pontardawe.

I had made my first Snooker century break, 101, on my seventeenth birthday, and won the Welsh Amateur Championship for the first time the same year, beating John Ford of Abertillery 5–3 in the final. I had lost 4–0 to him about three months previously in an exhibition so I was the underdog, but what people didn't know was that I had learned something very important from the drubbing he had given me. I was basically a potter but watching John, a master of the stun shot, control the cue-ball, gave me a clear idea of what I should be practising if I was going to improve. This made all the difference to my game and I went on to win the Welsh Championship six years in succession.

Coming from a family of miners, I had followed in father's footsteps and left school at fourteen to go down the local pit. Then, in 1954, I moved to Stoke in the Potteries to work at the Florence Colliery. The most memorable experience of my three years there was being buried alive for three hours when the top heading of the coalface caved in with me underneath it. I was literally unable to move an inch, not my fingers, my feet nor my face. If I tried to struggle in any way, my breathing passages became even more clogged than they were already. I was helpless.

It took twelve men three hours to get me out after shifting about four or five yards of rubble. I could hear them but hadn't any idea how they were getting on. I was afraid too that someone might break my fingers by sticking a shovel into them—which would have been very bad for my Snooker. In fact, the first part of me that I could move was the fingers of my left hand which I used to signal that I was alive.

Psychologically, my only brother, Ron, who is seventeen years younger than I am, had saved me. About this time we used to play marbles together, so, while I was buried there I played endless games of marbles with him in my mind. I suppose that it's only at times like these that you really realise how much you love and depend on your family. If I couldn't have focused on Ron and our games of marbles I'd have gone out of my mind.

I wasn't injured except for a burn mark across my neck from the girder and never had any trouble sleeping afterwards, as was expected. Happily, I didn't have any ill effects at all. However, the experience did nothing to recommend mining as a lifetime career so shortly afterwards I joined the police, a job I kept for seven years and eight months, long enough to learn a great deal about many aspects of life. At the same time, a policeman's life is never really his own, and the pay was not very exciting, though I had some great fun playing in the Police Snooker Championships which I won on most occasions when I entered.

Apart from the Welsh Championship, at this time I had also been entering the English Amateur Championship but, as Wales was allowed only one qualifier for this event, it was quite difficult even to get to London for the final stages. Cliff Wilson, who also came from Tredegar, was playing very well and beat me twice in the qualifying competition although, strangely enough, I always seemed to beat him in the Welsh.

When I did get through to London I couldn't seem to do justice to myself. The championship was played in Burroughes and Watts Hall in Soho Square, a venue with a plush, intimate atmosphere all its own and a beautiful-looking, very fast table that took a lot of getting used to. I had particular trouble potting into the middle pockets, but was fortunate enough to have this sorted out for me by George Orrell, who sold papers in Oxford Street just round the corner. George had only one arm but regularly used to get through a few rounds of the London qualifying section, being very knowledgeable and a keen follower of the game. Every year, as soon as I got to London, I would head straight for him and ask: 'George, who's the danger this year?'

It was George Orrell who told me that I was playing my pots into the middle pocket from the pink spot too slowly, which in any case was not my natural game, as I generally preferred to stun in this sort of shot. For some reason, I was playing differently at Burroughes. On most tables you can play for the far angle of the pocket and let the nap of the cloth pull the ball into the pocket but, as George pointed out, the strength of the nap seemed to vary from day to day. He just told me to aim at the biggest part of the pocket and use my natural stun game.

9

Having sorted out this particular difficulty, there were other deficiencies in my game which the ultra-fast table at Burroughes exposed. My safety play was very limited, often just aiming to return the cue-ball to somewhere near the baulk cushion without trying to place it where it might put my opponent in difficulties. I was also a bit too lax in that I didn't always take full advantage of an opening. All too often, I found out the hard way that it was no use making 20, 30, 40 or even 50 from an opening if I then missed and let my opponent back into the frame.

The higher the standard at which you compete, the more important it is NOT TO MISS WHEN YOU'RE IN. You must develop the killer instinct in this respect. Once you've got your opponent down, you must nail him.

I had one stroke of really bad luck in 1956 when I got to the English Amateur final and led Tommy Gordon 7–3 at the end of the first day: my tip came off with the first shot I played on the second day and I lost 11–9. The following season, I was beaten in the first round by Trevor Scott, then dropped out of the championship for several seasons.

I had to stabilise my game and decided that I wouldn't enter again unless I was going to win. I started to build up my long potting, working out ways of getting in. I don't believe in too much manoeuvring for an opening. If you ignore a possible chance and play safe, hoping to get a better chance later on, you may never get one. You've just got to get in and the only way you can do it sometimes is by bringing off one of those long ones.

The next time I entered this Championship was in 1964 when I beat a succession of opponents from the West Country and the Midlands to win the Southern Area, then played John Spencer, who had won the Northern Area, in the final at the Central Hall, Birmingham. We played two days, both afternoon and evening, and I can honestly say that neither before nor since have I played in such ludicrous conditions as we did in the afternoon. These were sunny April days and, having inspected the hall only at night, the officials had done nothing about blacking out its huge windows. At certain parts of the table, the sun was squarely in a player's eyes and the fact that I always wear a watch, which also caught the sun, was a further difficulty.

We were 5–5 at the end of the first day's play and John was in front 7–6 before I won the last two frames of the second afternoon session, making a 74 break in the last, to lead 8–7. John won the first frame at night and I won the next three to win 11–8. This was our first clash but far from our last!

One lucky event which grew out of the Amateur Championship was a trip to South Africa with Jonathan Barron to play a test series. Jon and I won the first test 2–1 (with me losing to Jimmy Van Rensburg 4–2), lost the second 4–0, and won the decider 4–0. We had a fantastic welcome everywhere we played. There were full houses of 500–600 in each centre and the standard of opposition we encountered was high, much higher than I had expected. We received a lot of publicity and I made four centuries in exhibition matches.

The most important consequence of this trip was that it offered a possible way of becoming a professional. At that time, the professional game in Britain was something of a closed shop. There were no tournaments, no sponsors and less than half-a-dozen professional players. These took the view, short-sightedly I believe, that the more professionals there were, the more their earnings would be reduced. I thought then, and still do, that new professionals—provided that they play and conduct themselves well—are a great asset to the game. We now have more professionals than there have ever been and the game is booming as it has never boomed before.

While I was in South Africa, Ken Shaw of Union Billiards told me that he thought I had a future in Snooker and that if I decided to turn professional he would organise a tour to start me off. Without this encouragement, I doubt whether I would have had the courage, although this was also the time when first John Spencer and then Garry Owen took the plunge. The difference between us was that, at that time, John had no career to give up, was not married and had had a row with the Billiards Association. Gary, having won two World Amateur Championships, had gone as far as he could go as an amateur and, in any case, only played professional part-time to start with as he retained his job as a fireman in Birmingham.

I was determined either to make Snooker my one and only livelihood or to stay an amateur. The chance of returning to South Africa was the deciding factor but I really struggled when I returned to England. After being welcomed to the Professional Association I was assured in no uncertain terms that I could expect no assistance. 'Everyone's on their own,' I was told. The one quarter from which some help was forthcoming was Riley Burwat, the table and equipment firm, who gave Spencer, Owen and myself small retainers.

I was determined not to take on cheap jobs for £5 or fees of that order. It was obvious that I could get plenty of work for nothing or next to nothing, but I was determined to set a standard and stick to it. The net result of all my efforts was that after eighteen months as a professional I had £8 in the bank!

My debut in the World Professional Championship was at Stoke in February 1969 when, in a 47 frame quarter-final, Fred Davis beat me 25–24. The match contained some of the longest sessions ever seen. The Thursday evening session finished at a quarter to one in the morning; the Friday afternoon session, which started at 2/45 finished at 7/30.

I had started this session three frames behind but I ended it two in front, the last frame of the session being in progress 35 minutes before a ball was potted. I won the first frame of the final session but Fred, taking no chances at all, won the next four to go one in front with two to go. I levelled the match at 24–24 but Fred took the decider at 1/33 am to win 25–24. I learned so much from this match that I didn't feel too disappointed at losing. The tactical battle with such a master as Fred was thoroughly enjoyable and I'm sure that this defeat equipped me all the better for the future.

As it happens, I drew him again the following year and this time, with all that valuable experience behind me, I beat him quite comfortably and went on to beat Spencer 39–34 in the semi-final.

This match aroused some controversy at the time because it was played on an unusually tight table. Certain pots which would have been easy on most tables had to be played with great care or ignored altogether, thus posing problems of frustration and self-discipline for both of us. I adapted my game quite a lot to these conditions but at vital stages I still went for the pot whenever I could instead of playing safe.

My final against John Pulman was a strange encounter in that for most of the match it looked as if I would win by the proverbial mile, only for John to dig his heels in and restrict my final margin to a mere 37–33.

At 27–14 I was 13 frames in front but my concentration must have lapsed for a while and, as John regained some of his touch, I started to struggle. Winning 5–1 on Friday afternoon, 4–2 on Friday night and 4–2 on Saturday afternoon, John was only 32–34 adrift going into the final session. He won the first frame at night with a 62 break to make it 34–33 and led 30–24 in the next frame as he put me in difficulty with a safety shot.

Fortunately, I could just squeeze one red past another into the top pocket, and then rolled the cue-ball up dead behind the green to land John in trouble. There was no way he could avoid letting me in and a 38 break enabled me to clinch the frame. This was 35–33, and the turning point, as I won the next two frames for the match and prize money of £1,125.

The World Champion normally holds his title for twelve months but an offer from Australia to stage the event in November, only six months later, meant that I was soon in the thick of it once more. I had time to make a tour of South Africa and started well enough in my title defence in Australia, beating both Eddie Charlton and John Spencer 21–16 to qualify for the semi-finals with an unbeaten record.

The system of running the Championship was strange in that it was neither round robin nor knock-out, but a combination of the two. Added to this, the draw was changed for the semi-finals. After it had been announced that I was to play Warren Simpson and Spencer was to play Charlton, I was suddenly informed that I was playing Spencer. Not unnaturally, I was in completely the wrong frame of mind for the match and lost 34–15.

Back home I had the satisfaction of winning the Park Drive £600 tournament by beating Spencer 4–0 in the final, making a 127 break in the final frame, and also the £750 first prize in the Park Drive £2,000 (after needing a snooker in the final frame) by beating Spencer 4–3.

Sandwiched between these, however, was a 25–23 loss to Rex Williams in the quarter-final of the 1971–2 Championship. Somewhat rashly, I agreed to play our 49 frame match in several Scottish club venues, most of which proved to be on extremely tight tables. I failed to adapt sufficiently and so went out.

The rest of the season consisted of the usual round of one-night stands. These may sound dull when compared with championships and tournaments but I never regard them as such since every audience is different and I have to start from scratch each night to produce the quality of play which justifies my fee. During the summer, for the second time, I played exhibitions all week at Pontins' Holiday Camps, starting on Mondays at Lowestoft on the East Coast and working my way round to Brean Sands in the South West by Fridays.

One day at the Broadreeds camp I gave them—and myself— something to remember when I took all fifteen reds, fifteen blacks and all the colours for the maximum break of 147. (See appendix, page 126.) Oddly enough, not long afterwards I scored another maximum as I took blacks with the first thirteen reds. Then, just as I was taking a red into the top pocket, a face bobbed up behind it: in the family atmosphere, a little boy had crawled under the table!

Looking back, all the dashing about I did that summer was not the best preparation I could have had for the 1972–3 season. I was third out of four in the Park Drive £2,000 though I made a break of 146 against Pulman (taking a pink after the ninth red) which was and is the highest break ever made in a professional tournament.

By now, all sorts of smaller professional tournaments had sprung up with John Spencer, Alex Higgins, John Pulman and myself playing for three days or a week wherever there was a promoter willing to chance his arm. In Birmingham I lost to Pulman 7–6 in the final after leading 4–0 but I won tournaments in Southampton and the Isle of Wight, the one venue which proved to be something of a disaster.

In fact, we had now arrived at a situation, where instead of automatically giving preference to tournaments over exhibitions, I was having to become more choosy, something which had seemed quite unlikely ever in my early days as a professional. Some of these tournaments, of course, were well worth playing in, like the 'Men of the Midlands' where I lost 5–3 in the final to Higgins. I had earlier beaten Higgins twice in the round-robin section of the tournament and had, in fact, won five of my six matches, but my loss in the final showed that I was still not playing as consistently as I would have liked, though I was playing much better than I had been at the start of the season.

The World Championship was staged in Manchester in April with a completely new set-up, two big arenas for the main matches and six smaller rooms for the others. This proved to be a great success from the sponsors', promoters' and public's point of view, but it did pose some new problems for the players.

I started with a match against Jim Meadowcroft in one of the smaller rooms, just over the cafeteria, so that the noise from there and of the people marching from one match to another made it a bit like playing in the middle of Piccadilly Circus. Nevertheless, I was able to shut myself off from all the distractions when I really needed to and won 16–10 to go into the quarter-final. With only four tables in use, concentration was easier and an 8–0 whitewash in the second session put me well on the road to a 16–6 win over Gary Owen.

The semi-final against Spencer was an extraordinary match. For the first time, I was playing in one of the big arenas with Eddie Charlton and Alex Higgins playing the other semi-final in the other. For the first three days, the public was more interested in seeing Eddie hammer Alex, which he did to the tune of 23–9. I felt a bit as if I was playing in a vacuum, a cold one at that, and let slip several frames I should have won. When I was 12–18 down in our 45 frame match, my odds, which had started at 10–1, had lengthened to 100–1, particularly since I lost the first frame on the third day. I won the next two to make it 14–19 but the real turning point came in the next frame when John missed an easy black which, instead of putting him 20–14, six in front, put me 15–19, only four behind.

Just then, the Charlton/Higgins match finished on the other table and with a full house now watching my game and no extraneous crowd noises to distract me, I could feel the adrenalin starting to flow. I won the last two frames of the afternoon session (making five in a row) to make it 18–19 and made an 88 in the first frame at night to tie the match at 19–19. I was far from out of the wood as I was down again 20–21, but I was one up with two to go and eventually won the decider 79–7 to delight the faithful few who had backed me when I had been 100–1.

Almost inevitably, I suffered a reaction when I started the 75 frame final against Charlton the next day as I lost the afternoon session 0–7! I took the next three sessions 5–2, 5–3, 7–1 to lead 17–13 but, as I fully expected, Eddie was very difficult to nail. His range of shots is slightly more limited than that of the other top players, but within this range he is very consistent and keeps the game so tight that he is liable to nag his opponent into errors.

I was unable to increase my lead and Eddie fought back twice to only one behind before the eighth session broke the pattern. Leading 27–25 at the start of this, I was surprised to discover that we were now playing under very intense additional lighting which had been brought in by the BBC, who were now filming. Eddie, who has protuberant eyebrows and heavy-lidded eyes, wasn't affected but I just couldn't see properly. Before I knew what was happening, I had lost three in a row and was one behind. By the mid-session interval I was very unhappy and a few words were exchanged in the tournament director's office. Joe Davis happened to be there and I was glad he was because after it had been agreed that two of the largest floodlights, which in any case were needed only to light the crowd, would be extinguished, he advised me to wait a few minutes and

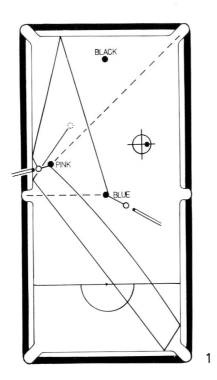

1

simmer down before I started playing again.

This sound advice helped me recapture the lead to go into the last day with a 31–29 advantage. I now felt confident that, having surmounted this unexpected crisis, I would win while Eddie, it was obvious next day, had cracked. I won the afternoon session 5–2 and eventually wrapped it up in the evening session 38–32.

Of course, it was a lovely feeling to win, not quite the elation perhaps of winning the title for the first time, but a deeper satisfaction because it was not until I lost the title that I realised how much I treasured it.

After the Championship, I felt no let down as I won a big tournament on Yorkshire TV the following week, made a record 68 centuries on my tour of South Africa, and in autumn 1973 made my second 147 at Bushey Conservative Club, Herts, a break in which the worst crisis did not come until the very end, when, in potting the blue, I failed to dislodge the pink as much as I had intended from its awkward position near the cushion (figure 1). Cue-ball and pink finished only an inch or so apart which makes potting angles difficult to judge. Nevertheless, I played the shot sharply with right-hand side and brought the cue-ball off three cushions to leave not a perfect, but a good enough, position to pot the black for the 147, a great satisfaction in itself, but in some strange way an incentive to do it again. I have since made three more maximums.

I retained my world title in 1974 but in circumstances which made it, for me, an anticlimax. I was braced for a titanic struggle which never materialised as John Spencer, Eddie Charlton and Alex Higgins who, in their different ways, represented the three main threats, all lost in or before the quarter-finals. The only hint of resistance I experienced was from Marcus Owen in the quarters. We were level at 8–8 but I won 15–11 and went on to beat Fred Davis 15–3 in the semi-final and Graham Miles 22–12 in the final.

The next twelve months were incredibly hectic with trips to India and South Africa as well as three big sponsored tournaments, the Pontins Professional in May, which I won, the Norwich Union Open, in which I lost 9–8 to John Spencer in the final, and the Benson and Hedges Masters when Spencer beat me 10–9 on a re-spotted black in the final frame!

I was playing quite well but the incessant travelling and playing was impairing my feeling for the game so that my concentration was sometimes patchy. For this reason, I gave myself the luxury of a whole week off before I started my defence of the title in Australia with a match against Warren Simpson, a very experienced local player. I was very rusty at the start but won 15–11 to qualify for the quarter-final against Spencer.

This in itself created a big controversy because it seemed ludicrous that Spencer was seeded as low as no 8 since he had beaten me in two major tournaments that season and has twice won the world title. The seedings were meant to depend on the previous year's championship, in which Spencer had unexpectedly lost in the last 16 to Perrie Mans of South Africa, but even this system was not strictly adhered to.

I was not very happy about meeting my closest rival as early as the last 8 and there were many comments in the press and inside the game to the effect that the seedings were a farce. As it happened, the World Professional Billiards and Snooker Association changed the seeding system for world championships a few months later but at the time Spencer and I just had to make the best of it.

In the event, we produced what we later agreed was the best match we ever have played and perhaps one of the best matches of all time. Neither of us had ever potted better or defended better and there must have been at least a dozen frames won from 50 or 60 behind.

John made two centuries, 103 and 114, in taking the opening session 4–2 and went on to lead 7–3 and 10–6 before I got in front 12–11. We were level at 15–15 and John was in front 17–16 before I won the next three frames to win 19–17.

From 10–10, I beat Alex Higgins 19–14 in the semi final to qualify to play Eddie Charlton in the final at the Nunawading Basketball Stadium, Melbourne.

When I won the third session 6–0 to lead 12–6 and extended this lead to 16–8, I thought I was more or less home and dry, but Eddie is a great fighter and won the next nine frames to lead 17–16.

I managed to win the last three frames on the third evening to lead 19–17 and maintained this lead to 22–20 on the fourth afternoon. The fourth evening, however, brought a 5–1 for Eddie and a 25–23 overnight lead which he increased to 28–23 (making a sequence of eight in a row) by taking the first four on the last day.

I took the last two frames of this session with breaks of 60 and 59, clearing the table in the latter with the aid of a neck or nothing pink, to keep in the match at 25–29. If I had missed that pink it would almost certainly have been 30–24 to Eddie, who would thus have needed only one of the last seven frames to become champion. Normally unemotional outwardly, Eddie wilted visibly when that pink went in, and his composure and confidence were further undermined by the desperate finish to the first frame of the final session.

Eddie was 19 in front on the green and produced a magnificent pot to lead by 22 with only the last four colours remaining. He needed to pot only the brown from its spot from a position in which he would pot it nine times out of ten but, under the tension of the moment, left the brown in the jaws for me to take the last four balls to tie the frame.

I lost the toss for the re-spotted black and left Eddie two half chances to pot it, from the second of which he not only overcut the black but went in-off to lose the frame.

Although there was still a long way to go, I felt that this was the psychological moment when Eddie lost the match. I won the next four frames to extend my winning streak to seven to lead 30–29 before Eddie broke the sequence to level at 30–30, leaving the match dependent on the very last frame.

Early in the decider, Eddie twice had me in terrible trouble but eventually I managed to compile a break of 62 which enabled me to retain the title and take the £4,000 first prize.

Being World Champion gives me an extra pride of performance. Far from relaxing when I have won the title, it offers me a new incentive. Champion or not, I always try my hardest in any engagement but, if things are not going well, if the conditions are bad or if I'm not feeling like it, I tell myself: 'Come on, you're the Champion, show them something good.'

The 1976 Championship, sponsored by Embassy, was held in two venues, the top half of the draw—mine—being played at Middlesbrough Town Hall and the other half at Wythenshaw Forum, Manchester, where Alex Higgins scored three close wins to qualify to meet me in the final.

At Middlesbrough, I played as well as I have ever done, beating John Dunning 15–7, Dennis Taylor 15–2 and Perrie Mans, the first South African ever to reach the semi-final, 20–10. It was not very satisfactory for me to play three matches in one venue on an excellent table and then to play the final in a completely different environment at Wythenshaw Forum on a table which I felt justified in complaining about very strongly.

The match also started badly when, in the first session, the television lighting produced so much glare and dazzle that I could not see properly. The lights were re-arranged but what with this and the bad table I didn't play anything like my best.

My opponent was also affected, I think, though he coped better than I did in the early stages. At 11–11 and even when I was only two frames in front at 15–13 he was well in the match point, but when I won the next frame from 0–68 and also both the following frames from behind, his resistance crumbled. I won quite comfortably 27–16 earning £6,000 first prize to add to the £2,000 I had earned by winning the Benson & Hedges Masters just before, and the £1,000 first prize I won two weeks later from the Pontins Professional tournament at Prestatyn.

I love playing Snooker for a living but the general public have little idea of what a professional's life actually entails. 'Pot Black', a tournament I've won once and lost in the final twice, provides in a sense, Snooker's showcase, worlds away from the slog of one-night stands in clubs up and down the country, hospitable and friendly as they invariably are. Occasionally, their eagerness to please back-fires. There was one club where I noticed that the cloth was a peculiar colour. 'Oh yes,' said the secretary, 'it was looking a bit dirty so we had it dry cleaned.'

At another club, in South Africa, I was having trouble keeping my balance on a slippery floor. I mentioned this and during the interval someone sprinkled Ajax all over it. For five minutes everything was fine but as I started to disturb the Ajax great clouds of it started to rise. Very soon, everyone was making for the door, eyes streaming and handkerchieves clutched in their hands.

* * *

As the game continues to grow, so will the strain on the top players become more severe. Like golfers and tennis players, Snooker professionals are having to accustom themselves to a tough intercontinental schedule, for Snooker is expanding so fast in Australia, New Zealand, South Africa, Canada, India and many other countries that some tempting rewards are now available. The pursuit of these rewards is often exhausting but I will never let it become so much so that it diminishes my enjoyment of the game. Without that enjoyment, few professional sportsmen could function. I certainly couldn't.

18

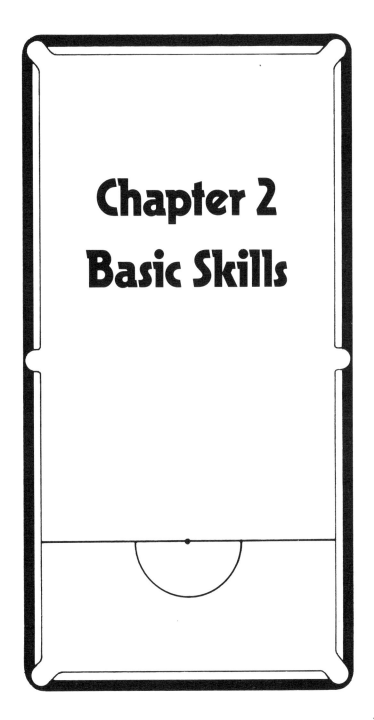

Chapter 2
Basic Skills

I have been playing Snooker for twenty-five years and without a doubt the game is more popular now than it has ever been. Most estimates put the number of the players in the British Isles alone at about three and a half million, so I have no idea what the figure would be if the bigger Snooker playing nations like Australia, South Africa and Canada were included.

A lot of the game's present interest in this country stems from the BBC2 'Pot Black' series which brought Snooker to the homes of millions of people who previously had only a hazy idea of what it was all about. One of the effects of this was to send sales of miniature tables rocketing; another was to establish the faces of the leading players with the general public as well as the hard core of Snooker followers.

But despite all this extra public exposure, the proportion of good players remains lower than in almost any other sport. Coaching is less readily available so one generally finds promising players coming from towns where there are already many good players to observe and learn from. Many people play regularly for forty years or more without improving much because the various spins and positional stratagems remain an unexplained mystery to them.

Actually, there is very little mystique about it. I think that in five minutes I could show any player who has played a few games how to screw the cue-ball back and stop it dead. The same applies to the other Snooker skills. All that is needed to master them is some basic ball sense and co-ordination and the small initial effort necessary to master anything new.

Right at the start let me say that no one can reach his full potential without buying his own cue. I recommend a grained ash cue of between 16 and $17\frac{1}{2}$ ounces although I have seen plenty of good players using other types of cue. The important thing is to get one cue and stick to it.

Any good amateur or professional will tell you that every cue behaves differently and that they always play with the same cue wherever they go. It is not particularly important even to play with a straight cue. John Pulman's and John Spencer's are both bent like the proverbial dog's hind leg but this does not matter as they can only see the first eighteen inches of their cue as they play their shots. As players become accustomed to the feel of a particular cue, they tend always to hold it in exactly the same place. In this way, both Spencer and Pulman play with their bent cues 'straight way up'.

My own cue has a slight bend in it but it has never worried me. What worried me far more in the 1971–2 season was when it split at the top. I couldn't play with it, nor could I play with anything else, but in the end a stroke of delicate surgery lopped two inches from the top and added two inches to the butt. The shaft was sandpapered down until the thickness of the cue where it rests on my bridge hand was about the same as before and eventually I started to play well again. I play with a ten millimetre tip and my cue measures 4 feet 8 inches, which is roughly the length favoured by most top amateurs and professionals.

What puts a lot of keen players off instructional books is too much dogmatic direction. Logically, the orthodox way may seem best but this is only because the good orthodox players outnumber the good unorthodox ones. It's also worth remembering that even the so-called orthodox players have small parts of their game which look unorthodox. So while the ambitious player should be aware of what is generally regarded as 'correct' and 'incorrect' he should never be afraid of trusting his instinct and cutting across generally accepted methods.

In my own case, those on the inside of the Snooker scene agree that my own stance is eccentric in that my elbow juts outwards at an angle to the cue whereas, with most good players, one could draw a straight (or nearly straight) line between cue, elbow and the point of the shoulder. As it happens, I broke my shoulder when I was a lad, but in any case people's arms and shoulders vary in shape and just do not fit into a so-called classic mould.

What really matters is delivering the cue through straight. On the face of it, those players who have perfect alignment start with an advantage here but the shape of your shoulder or any number of other factors can make this perfect alignment so difficult to acquire that it is a mistake to try. At all times, Snooker should be fun and it is no fun if you concentrate on contorting yourself into strange shapes before you even hit the ball. In any case, I don't think this does any good; you will merely crush the natural ability out of yourself. I think, with all due modesty, I pot a ball pretty well despite my jutting elbow. In short, as long as you deliver your cue straight it doesn't matter twopence where your elbow or your shoulder are.

On the other hand, there are certain 'rules', whatever your style, that are only commonsense to observe. Keeping your head down and keeping still on the shot is imperative. However modest your standard of play, this is one way of ensuring that you are at least making the most of whatever ability you have.

On my journeys round the clubs I see the same faults time after time. There's 'Spring-heeled Jack' who is so impatient to see what has happened to his shot that his head, and most of his body as well, shoots up before he has even hit the ball. 'Tango Fred', a split second after he has hit the ball, shuffles his feet either to the right or left according to where he wants it to go, and 'Tilting Bill' on an angle shot leans either to left or to right, as if he's looking round the corner, even while he's playing the shot.

Next there's 'Mr Spooner' who addresses the bottom of the cue-ball for every shot and then levers his cue upwards to hit the centre of the ball or even above, while 'Mr Fingers' holds the cue delicately with thumb and finger as if it's a piece of lettuce, not realising that it is impossible to screw back or play any forcing shot with such a light grip. 'The Snarler's' concentration as he addresses the cue-ball is so intense that his nose wrinkles, his mouth is half open and his eyes squint. His whole body is as tense as a spring so that he can't possibly build up a relaxed rhythm.

There is 'Tripod Harry' who stands absolutely square to the table, and finally, there is 'The Herculean Chalker' who rubs chalk on to his cue so furiously that great clouds of it form in the air and powder the floor. His tip becomes so encrusted with chalk that most of it is deposited on the cue-ball on impact, particularly if the atmosphere is slightly damp. It should be sufficient just to give your tip one firm wipe with your chalk. If it takes any more than that either your tip is not holding the chalk as it should or the chalk you are using is too powdery or too greasy.

Not only do these types of mannerisms recur the world over, so do the questions I am asked. Not a week goes by without my being asked whether I look at the cue-ball or the object-ball at the moment I am attempting a pot, or whether it is a good guide to potting to hit the object-ball 'where it shines'.

'Hitting it where it shines' is just an old wives' tale. 'Eye on which ball?' is a more important question though it can be taken too seriously.

Obviously at some stage, a player must look at both the cue-ball (to determine where his tip is going to strike it) and at the object-ball (to estimate the angle at which the cue-ball must contact it). I have heard some theories about switching the eyes from cue-ball to object-ball in a rhythm which synchronises with the cue sliding backwards and forwards but in my opinion this is valueless if it doesn't come naturally. If you concentrate on applying a theory like this, you will have no concentration left for potting. If a method is not natural it will take effort to apply it. The more complex the method, the more effort and concentration is needed—and you require all that concentration for potting and controlling the cue-ball.

Some methods do become ingrained so that after a time you use them naturally, but under pressure something acquired artificially tends to go wrong more easily than something which is natural. In a match, you need to direct all the concentration at your disposal towards winning. If any of that concentration is needed for preserving an unnatural element in your game, you will be at a disadvantage.

I know that when I actually strike the cue-ball my eyes are on the object-ball but beyond that I couldn't tell you at what stages my eyes switch between cue-ball and object-ball. Frankly, it's something which doesn't interest me and even when I've been playing badly I've not fallen into the trap of trying to work more 'system' into this aspect of my game.

There is a difference between trying to acquire a new method and simply cultivating good habits. One habit which I recommend is to walk to the table on the line of the shot so that when you take up your stance you are naturally sighting the object-ball at an angle to pot it. In other words, start to assess the angle of the shot as you are approaching the table and take your stance accordingly, rather than leave it until you are down on the shot and then needing to make radical adjustments of aim.

When your opponent misses, you should be thinking about what to do as you walk to the table. If you get down for your shot before you have decided what you are going to do, your indecisive state of mind will produce

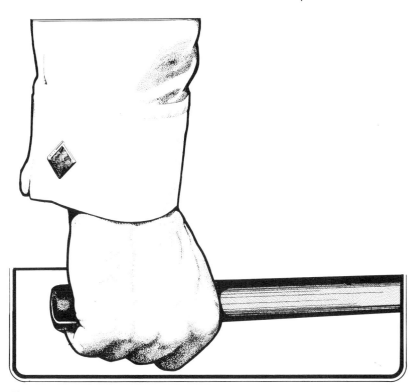

Figure 2 The grip

technical faults. What happens is that to alter the angle a player just changes the position of the cue and arm but not the position of his feet. This leaves him hitting across the ball and off balance.

The Grip

The correct grip is one which even beginners adopt quite naturally. It is common to see Tennis novices grip the racket (incorrectly) as if it was a frying pan but for Snooker nearly everyone seems to pick the cue up instinctively as if it was a poker or hammer (figure 2). It should be gripped a couple of inches from the butt (thick) end so that it fits snugly into the palm of the hand.

When you actually settle down to play your shot the line from your wrist to your elbow should be vertical or near vertical though, as I have already explained, there are some players, myself included, whose arms or shoulders have a slightly unusual feature which prevents this.

Figure 3 The stance, side view

The Stance

The details of a stance may vary but there are certain basics which all good players observe (figures 3 and 4).

Stand sideways to the table with your left foot (the leading leg for right handers) pointing in much the same direction as your cue. This front leg is bent. Your rear leg acts as a brace and should be straight. Some good players play with their right foot almost directly behind their left (ie facing perfectly sideways) whereas others, myself included, play with the right foot slightly to the right so that they are slightly more 'chest on' to the shot. The self-appointed purists may claim that the latter method is inferior to the former but I believe that as long as one's stance is comfort-

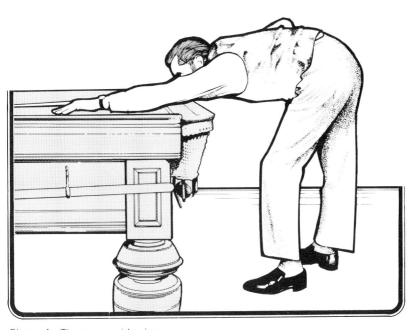

Figure 4 The stance, side view

able and firm, then there is unlikely to be much wrong with it.

A fair test to apply to your stance is to get a friend to give you a slight shove. If you stagger and almost fall over, you can safely assume that your stance is not solid enough. If, however, you just sway slightly then you are probably all right.

In the old days, some well known Billiards players used to play with both knees bent. They were able to get away with this because Billiards to some extent calls for less accuracy than Snooker and contains fewer forcing shots. Playing a forcing shot with knees bent, the body is more likely to move than if the rear leg is locked and firm. Your weight should be on your front foot.

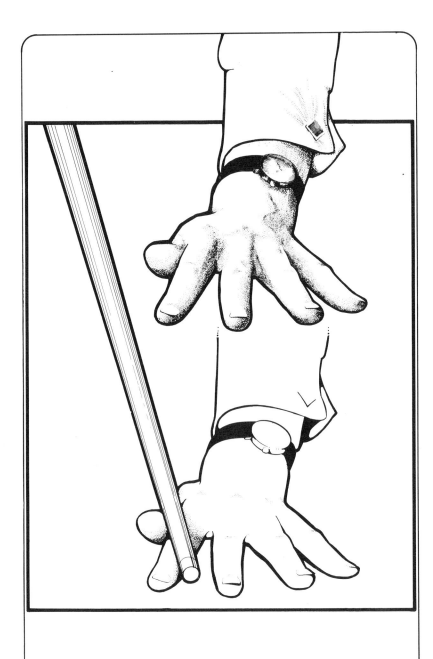

Figure 5 Forming the basic bridge

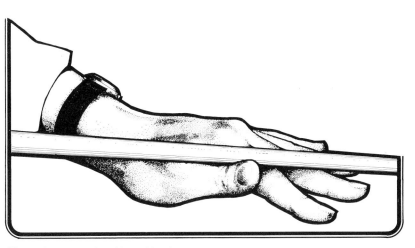

Figure 6   The basic bridge, side view

Bridging

To form the basic bridge, stand sideways to the table and place your left hand on the cloth, spreading the fingers widely and cocking the thumb (figure 5). This cocked thumb and the first finger form a channel in which the cue can be placed and through which it can pass gently backwards and forwards to prepare for and then play your shots.

The lower drawing in figure 5 is identical to the one above save that the cue has actually been placed in the bridge. Note that the cue not only passes through the channel described above but also over part of the first finger. This gives the bridge extra stability. When you are about to play your shot lean forward, bending from the waist as well as the front knee, so that the cue remains parallel to the bed of the table, as shown in the side view of the basic bridge (figure 6).

Some purists say that the bridge arm should be pushed out as straight as possible but most players find it more comfortable to play with it slightly bent (see the front view of the bridge and stance in figure 7).

When you have settled down to play a shot you will find that the cue is just brushing your upper chest and even your tie. This may help you psychologically to deliver the cue through straight. Your back (right) arm should be vertical to the ground so that, as you swing back and forth in addressing the ball, it should go first behind the vertical and then in front.

Physically, the elbow is like a hinge and an unnatural movement is produced if the position of the arm at rest is either in front of the vertical, which is rare, or behind it, as it is with quite a lot of ordinary players. These players hold the cue so far back that the arm from the wrist to elbow is way past the vertical and they cannot possibly play forcing shots well because they cannot draw the cue back without almost

Figure 7 The bridge and stance, front view

straightening the arm. This means that the cue scoops downwards into the cue-ball. Having the arm vertical from wrist to elbow and then swinging it back and forth like a pendulum gives you the best chance of level cueing—indeed, without it, I don't think you have much chance of anything but very limited success.

It is important to cultivate a follow-through for, without one, a stroke

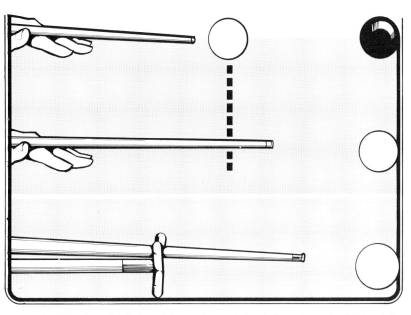

Figure 8 The shot. (top) the address; (centre) the follow-through; (bottom) the address using the rest

turns into a jab. In the top drawing in figure 8, I am preparing to play a stroke. The lower drawing shows the distance of my follow through. The tip should go through the cue-ball straight and clean as if it was a bubble. If the tip's contact with the cue-ball alters, even fractionally, on impact the direction in which the cue is travelling, it means that you are not cueing truly.

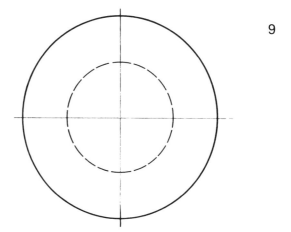

Striking

Everyone knows that the cue-ball is struck with the tip of the cue. What sort of tip does your cue have? Is it flat or domed? Spongy or shiny? Thin or thick?

The surface of the ball is round. Therefore, the tip can only strike a certain area of the ball. In figure 9 this is shown by the inner dotted line. Figure 10, a side view of the tip striking at the centre, bottom and top of the cue-ball, shows this target area from another angle and illustrates why your tip should be domed so that as much of its surface as possible is in contact with the cue-ball at the moment of impact. If your tip is flat, you will be striking at the round ball with a sharp flat edge and will tend to miscue frequently.

Your tip should not be spongy since it will tend to sink so much into the cue-ball at the moment of impact that crisp clean striking will be impossible. Neither should it be hard and shiny since it cannot grip the ball well enough to impart any spin without fear of a miscue.

While it is true that spongy tips sometimes 'bed down' into tips of just the right resilience, those which are hard and shiny to begin with never become softer, although one can temporarily offset the hardening of a tip by pressing the flat edge of a file into it or by gently roughening its surface with a matchbox. Tips do not become domed of their own accord so sandpaper them into shape.

Figure 11 shows where the tip should strike the cue-ball for true and accurate cueing, slightly below centre on the horizontal axis and dead centre on the vertical axis. Here, I can imagine many good Snooker players who have first learned to play Billiards saying 'That's not right. Surely he means "slightly above centre".' My answer to this is that Billiards is a game in which plain ball striking or striking with a little 'top' on the cue-ball, plays a very important part—much more than it does in

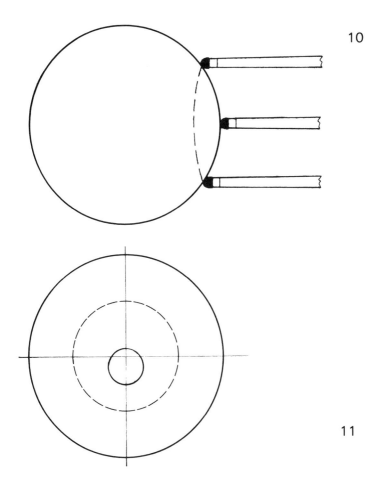

10

11

Snooker. Middle pocket and top pocket in-off are the foundation of Billiards and it is impossible to build up any consistency in this department unless you strike the cue-ball in the centre or slightly above it. But Snooker is a game of potting and you need a much greater degree of accuracy for pots than for in-offs.

There are several reasons for missing a pot. You may have assessed the angle at which you want the cue-ball to contact the object-ball incorrectly; you may have assessed the angle correctly but simply failed to make the intended contact; or the ball may 'roll off', that is, not run truly. It is to minimise the risk of the ball 'rolling off' that I recommend striking the cue-ball just below centre. In a sense, the benefit of this technique is only apparent when a player has progressed well beyond the novice stage, but since I am writing on the assumption that everyone wants to

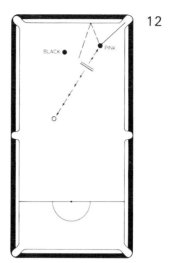

progress as far as this, it is as well to ingrain good habits right at the start.

When you strike below centre you are automatically applying backspin. This means that the ball is spinning backwards as it is propelled forward by the cue. The lower you hit the ball, the more backspin is applied. The purpose of using just a little backspin by striking just below centre is merely to enable you to play shots slightly harder than would be the case if you struck the cue-ball dead centre or just above, thus not giving the cue-ball time to 'roll off' before it reaches the object-ball.

In figure 12, the first five arrows are pointed backwards to denote that the cue-ball is spinning backwards up to the point marked //. The arrows pointing forward towards the object-ball illustrate that the normal forward motion of the cue-ball is now in force. The purpose of striking just below centre is to enable you to strike the cue-ball quite hard without having to strike the object-ball hard. To a good player, the effect of using this shot is in some ways almost to enable him to play the shot from the point marked // rather than from the cue-ball's original position. If this seems complicated, take this on trust for the time being. You'll appreciate the value of it later.

I have seen novices get down and strike the cue-ball first time with no preliminaries at all, but even the fastest professionals don't do that. There are no time limits in Snooker so there is no need to hurry. At the same time, if you take too long you will find yourself using so much concentration for easy shots that you won't be able to intensify it for shots which are more difficult, and will also find that you never build up an easy fluent rhythm.

What I have said so far will start beginners along the right lines and may well refresh the minds of better players whose game has perhaps suffered through losing sight of the importance of the basics.

Chapter 3
Supplementary Skills

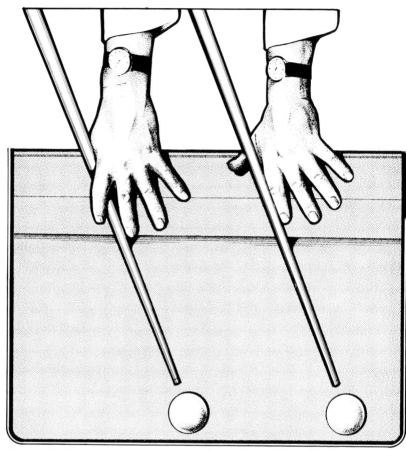

Figure 13 Supplementary bridges using the cushion rail, top view

Soon, however, it will become all too obvious that the standard bridge needs various modifications to cope with different positions. When the cue-ball is too close to the cushion to bridge at the correct length with the hand on the table, place the lower part of the hand from the knuckles to finger tips on the cushion rails as shown in figure 13. The body weight is forward, thus helping to make this bridge more solid. The back of the hand is below the level of the cushion rail. The path of the cue is kept

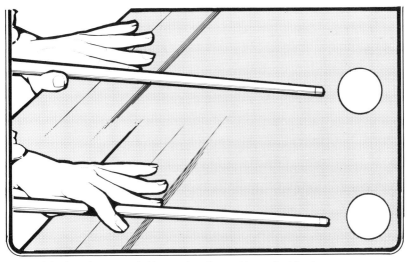

Figure 14 Supplementary bridges using the cushion rail, side view

straight by the channel formed by the thumb and first finger as seen in the illustration on the right in figure 13 but the stroke can also be made by using the 'tuck under' bridge shown on the left.

This bridge is made by tucking the thumb underneath the first finger and taking the first finger outwards so that the cue can run between it and the second finger. Figure 14 shows these two bridges from the side. The 'tuck under' bridge tends to be favoured when the cue-ball is slightly further from the cushion.

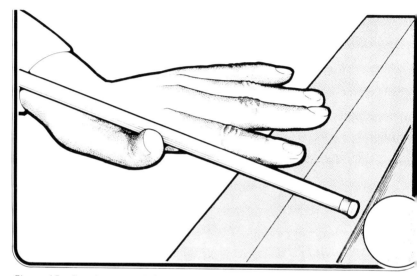

Figure 15 Supplementary bridge using the cushion rail

When the cue-ball is tight under the cushion, the left arm is straightened and supported on the cushion rails only by the tips of the fingers, as in figure 15. The cue is slightly raised to strike as low at the cue-ball as the cushion will permit, thus minimising the risk of a miscue.

Figure 16 shows two awkward bridges for shots when the cue has to travel parallel to a cushion. In the top illustration, the hand is tilted so that three fingers rest on the cushion rail while the thumb and first finger form a loop below the level of the cushion to allow a stroke to be made. The finger nearest the playing area acts as an additional aid to keeping the cue on a straight line.

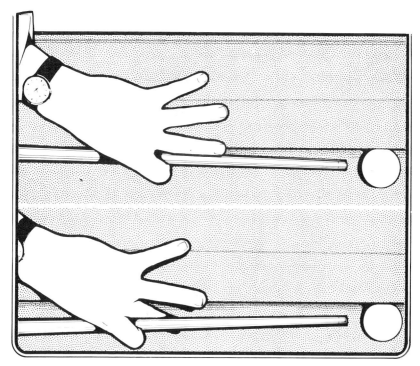

Figure 16 Supplementary bridges along the cushion rail

The lower illustration shows that it is sometimes possible to place another finger on the bed of the table to give the bridge extra stability. In this case, the cue runs across that finger, thus making it easier to keep the cue steady.

Not only does the bridge have to be varied but, often, the stance as well. As a Snooker table is twelve feet long you will need artificial aids (ie the rest) to reach certain shots and you will be unable to reach others without stretching or in some way modifying your stance.

Figure 17 Mounting the table, side view

Figure 17 shows a common position. Cue-ball and object-ball are too far over for you to adopt your natural stance. Many players in this situation balance on their left leg and lean over with their right leg in the air in what I call the 'dying swan' position, but it is difficult to remain steady poised like this and there is also the disadvantage that you will be pointing the cue downwards. There are times when you have no choice but to play like this (if, for instance, other balls are where you want to place your left leg) but, whenever possible, good players prefer to hoist their left leg on to the table and lie on the cushion with very little weight on the right foot which must, of course, remain in contact with the floor to make the shot legal.

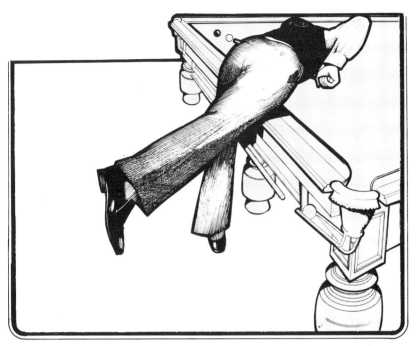

Figure 18   Mounting the table, back view

On the opposite side of the table, another kind of stretch is sometimes needed—in figure 18 my weight is entirely on my left leg though I am also, of course, leaning against the table to keep myself steady.

Some players prefer when possible to hoist their right knee on to the table not only to help them keep motionless on the shot but to keep their cue arm and shoulder more behind the line of the shot though, as my upper body is quite supple, I can stretch for these shots comfortably and without loss of accuracy.

NEVER be tempted to overstretch. It is much better to learn to use the rest (which no one can avoid altogether) than to trust to a shaky addressing of the cue-ball and a final desperate prod as you overbalance.

Figure 19   Using the rest, the grip

The Rest

When using the rest it is necessary to change from your normal 'hammer' grip of the cue to a sideways grip with the palm of the hand folded over the top of the cue (figures 19 and 20). Some players even place their palms squarely behind the butt of the cue. It is also necessary, of course, for the body to be behind the line of the shot (figure 20), or even to the left of it, so that your right shoulder is nearer the cue-ball than your left.

The arm from wrist to elbow should be horizontal and the power of the stroke should come from behind this lower arm. Make a smooth continuous stroke, hitting right through the cue-ball and keeping, as with all shots, your head down.

The rest itself should be firmly anchored to the table with your left

Figure 20 Using the rest, front view

hand. The way I hold the rest is adequate for me but some players feel there is an extra insurance against instability in placing the palm of the left hand on top of the rest.

Almost all amateurs use the rest the wrong way. Most use it tall-way up, whereas I believe it is more efficient to use it short-way up. One of the general principles of accurate striking of the cue-ball is that the cue should be as horizontal as possible to the table bed. If you use the rest tall-way up, the intersection in the rest head is far too high for any shot except one where you need to use a lot of top. The artificial bridge which the rest provides when used tall-way up means that, even for striking the cue-ball in the centre, the cue-tip is dragging downwards and almost certainly applying some sort of spin unintentionally.

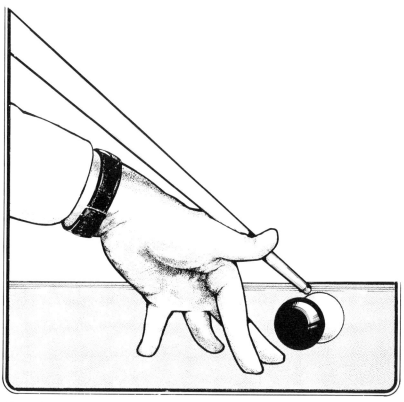

Figure 21   Bridging over a ball

Bridging over a Ball

The necessity of striking downwards is the root of the problems which arise from playing over an intervening ball. With an ordinary shot, you are looking almost horizontally along the line of the shot so that the cue-ball, object-ball and usually the pocket are all in the same line of vision. But in bridging over a ball (figures 21–24) it is a physical impossibility for the eyes to take in cue-ball, object-ball and pocket unless these are very close to each other because you are looking not horizontally, but downwards. Therefore, after assessing the shot, you usually have to remember where one is aiming, either on the cue-ball or the object-ball.

There are also the problems that your bridge cannot be as stable as it is with the ordinary bridge and that you can hit only the upper part of the cue-ball. Your first priority must be to avoid committing a foul stroke by touching the obstructing ball with your cue or fingers.

Figure 21 shows how to give yourself the best chance of a successful shot though in this awkward position it rarely pays to be too ambitious or

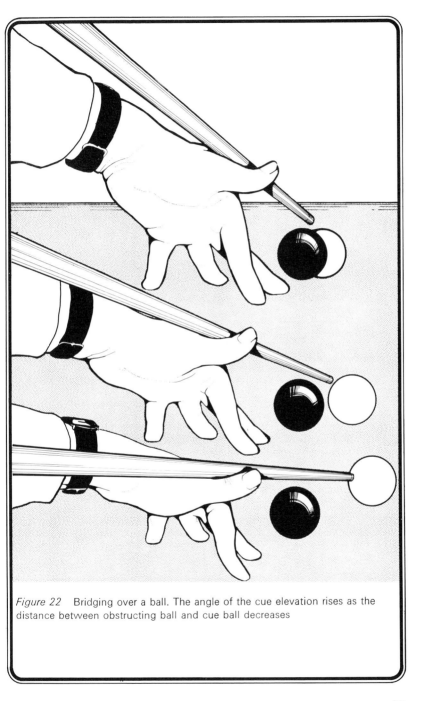

Figure 22   Bridging over a ball. The angle of the cue elevation rises as the distance between obstructing ball and cue ball decreases

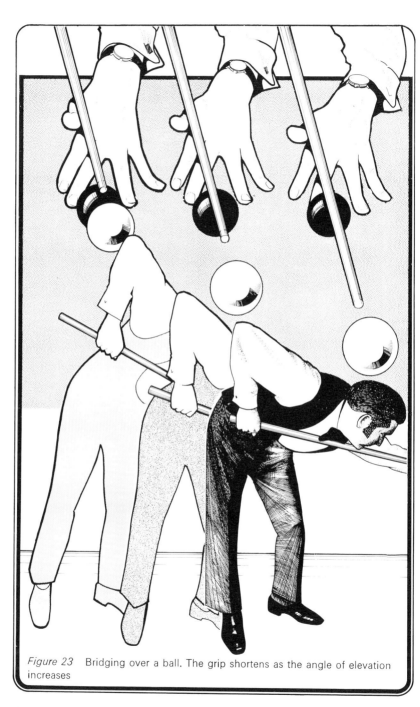

Figure 23 Bridging over a ball. The grip shortens as the angle of elevation increases

44

Figure 24 Mounting the table to bridge over a ball

to expect too much. Note that the fingers are widely spread for maximum stability with two fingers forward and two back. The front finger is within an inch or so of the obstructing ball. The weight is firmly forward so the bridge hand bears down on the table. The cue is elevated at an angle which enables it just to miss the obstructing ball as it plays at the top of the cue-ball.

The nearer the cue-ball is to the obstructing ball, the more difficult the shot becomes. As figure 22 shows, the angle of cue elevation needs to rise more steeply, the nearer the cue-ball is to the obstructing ball.

I also shorten my grip in relation to the degree to which I need to elevate my cue (figure 23). When the two balls are very close, as in the illustration on the left, my grip is very short. When the two balls are almost (but not quite) far enough apart to use my normal bridge, I grip my cue (see illustration on the right) almost in the normal position. Note too that the steeper the elevation the more my body strains upwards to get over the top of the shot.

Figure 24 shows me sitting on the cushion rail (keeping one foot on the floor, of course, to comply with the rules) to bridge over two interven-

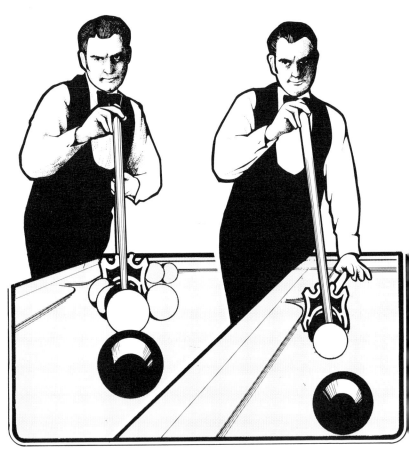

Figure 25 Using the spider. (left) other balls prevent the spider being laid on the table; (right) the preferred method

ing balls to pot a ball over the corner pocket, just out of picture.

In figure 25 I am using the spider, an implement designed like a rest except that the rest head is elevated. To use it, the same basic principles as those for bridging over an obstructing ball apply. Place the spider head as near as possible to the obstructing ball and elevate your cue to a degree sufficient to avoid a foul as you play at the cue-ball. Again, the distance between obstructing ball and cue-ball with be relevant to the angle of your cue elevation.

When you can, secure the spider on the table with your left hand on top of it (see right hand illustration) but when this is impossible hold it as still as you can as shown on the left.

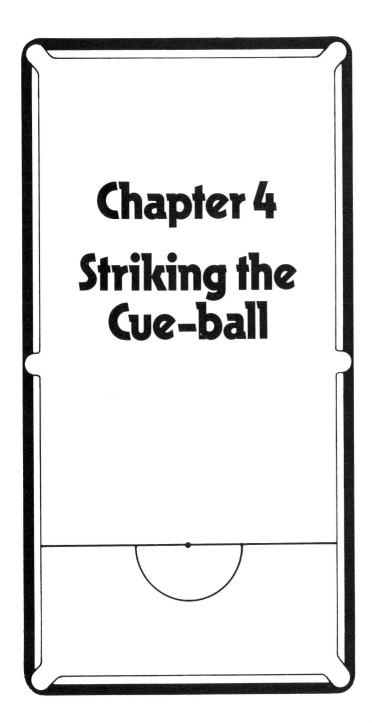

Chapter 4
Striking the Cue-ball

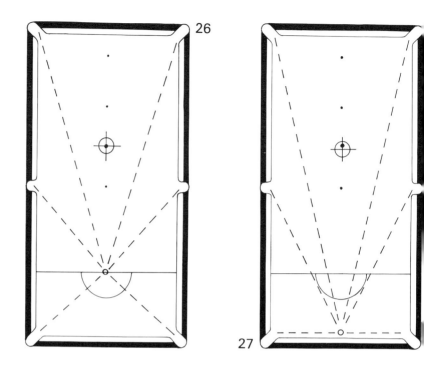

To set a novice on the right lines, place the cue-ball on the brown spot and get him to shoot into each of the six pockets in turn (figure 26). It should not cause him any great difficulty but a youngster's interest can often be caught in this way because the best results are obtained at this age by the achievement of simple things rather than by battling hopelessly to do something more difficult.

Figure 27, though, illustrates a more difficult shot since the cue-ball is placed on the middle of the baulk cushion so that there is an awkward bridge to contend with as well as a narrower angle to enter the pockets.

Tales are told of old-time professional Billiards players being locked away when they were young and told to practise with only one ball for an hour before they were allowed to practise with all three. Parents would find it difficult to impose such rigid discipline these days, nor would it necessarily have the intended results because the prime object of Snooker is enjoyment. Even a professional cannot function effectively unless he is enjoying the game. At the same time, there is a lesson in this emphasis on one-ball control.

Unless you can strike the cue-ball accurately you might ask yourself what chance you have of striking the object-ball accurately. If you strike the cue-ball perfectly in the centre it should run perfectly straight, but if you strike it a fraction to either side it will deviate from its course.

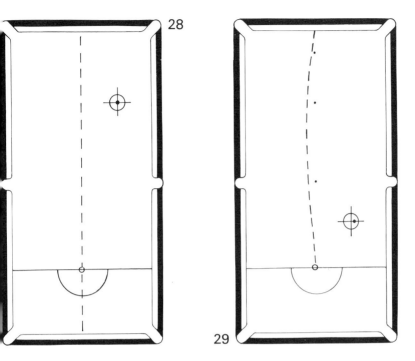

Figure 28 shows the exercise which all professionals have used and most still use to check their cueing. This is known as shooting over the spots. Place the cue-ball behind the brown spot and shoot over the blue, pink and black spots and back.

Play this shot steadily at first with just enough strength for the cue-ball to return to the baulk cushion. Even the novice should have little difficulty in playing up the table in a straight line but most of them will find, at least to start with, that the cue-ball returns either to the right or left of the spots because 'side' is being unintentionally applied.

So what is happening? Is your bridge hand wobbling as you deliver the cue through? Is your cue not coming through straight because your back arm is not coming through straight? Or, even worse, is your cue not aligned straight with the cue-ball in the first place?

On many tables, particularly the older type, there is a helpful guide available—a white spot exactly in the middle of the cushion rail. When you are practising shooting over the spots, glance down to ensure that your cue is covering this white spot. If it is not, you cannot be cueing absolutely straight.

Figure 29 shows what happens to the cue-ball when right-hand side is used. First, the cue-ball pushes out to the left but then swings back to the right. When left-hand side is used, of course, the converse happens: first

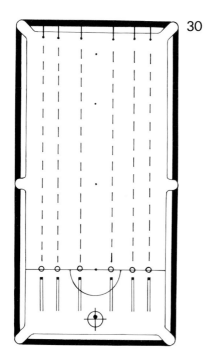

the cue-ball swings to the right and then to the left.

Obviously, with the cue-ball changing direction slightly twice, it is much more difficult to make precise contact on an object-ball several feet away than if the cue-ball proceeds in a straight line. It is true that experienced players, over a period of years, learn subconsciously to calculate the effects of side and address the cue-ball accordingly but it is necessary first to master plain ball striking so that any side which you may later feel it necessary to use is applied intentionally and not unintentionally. Therefore, work at shooting over the spots first at medium speed as already described, and then at greater speeds. As you hit the cue-ball harder, you will find it more difficult to avoid using some unintentional side.

When you strike the cue-ball hard enough for it to do four or five lengths you may initially find the cue-ball slipping sideways off the top cushion so that it finishes somewhere near the baulk pocket. Don't be discouraged by this. It is more difficult to be accurate with 'power' shots than with medium-paced shots, though this accuracy has to be acquired by ambitious players.

When playing at speed, make a special effort to keep the body still. Some club players almost swing themselves off their feet when playing a forcing shot. They swing their shoulder into the shot, their head comes shooting up and their cue finishes pointing into the light shade. Needless to say, these faults are all ruinous to accuracy. Make a special effort, however hard you are hitting the ball, to keep your cue firmly in your bridge at the completion of the shot. Concentrate on keeping your head motionless and you will find that this is the most important factor in keeping still as well.

It is unnecessary to wait until you have achieved utter perfection at shooting over the spots at all speeds before you progress to potting which, after all, is what the game is all about. I say this because there was one enthusiast with his own table who practised shooting over the spots so much that his table gradually developed a visible line. He became very proficient at this exercise but never made much progress at Snooker itself.

The lesson here is surely that one must never lose sight of the fact that practice is useful only in so far as it contributes to playing Snooker. It is valueless as an end in itself and it is a big mistake to become obsessed either with practice method or with fashioning a 'perfect' technique. For novices and good players alike, my advice is to eliminate drudgery from practice as much as possible but always practise with a purpose. Never knock the balls about aimlessly.

Another disadvantage of shooting over the spots too much is that you may get too accustomed to looking for the 'guidelines' of the blue and pink spots. Therefore try the matchstick exercise shown in figure 30. All you do here is to place six matchsticks with the ends projecting a fraction of an inch over the cushion. Fire up the table in a straight line at each in turn, trying to send the matchsticks flying on to the floor. Since the height of the cushion prevents any part of the cue-ball except the top contacting the matchstick, there is not an enormous margin of error with this exercise.

At all times try to hit the cue-ball smoothly. Make your preliminary addresses at the cue-ball rhythmically. Some players find it natural to bring the cue back a long way, others do not. In a sense, it does not matter what happens on the preliminary backswing in that it is only the final backswing and actual stroke which counts. However, most players whose preliminary addresses are short are suspect on forcing shots because the contrast between short preliminary swings and the long final swing necessary to hit a ball hard somehow seems to unbalance them. Therefore, it is best to cultivate an address which will allow you to feel natural whether you have to play relatively hard or relatively soft.

It is important that your preliminary addresses should feel free and easy. Some players' cue actions look as if they are sawing through a block of wood with a blunt saw. Sometimes, the tension of a match will make your action a bit stodgy, but when this happens stop for a second and let the muscles of your arm relax.

Most important of all is a slight hesitation at the end of the final backswing, rather like the way you see a top golfer pause at the top of his swing. If he took the club back fast and attempted to swing forward without any pause he would fall flat on his back. The Snooker player won't, but he will have a jerk in his action so drastic that his chances of improvement are nil.

Slowly back—slight pause—firmly through: that should be your motto.

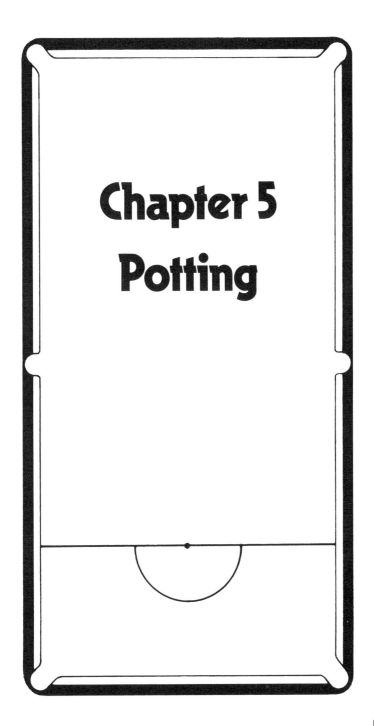

Chapter 5
Potting

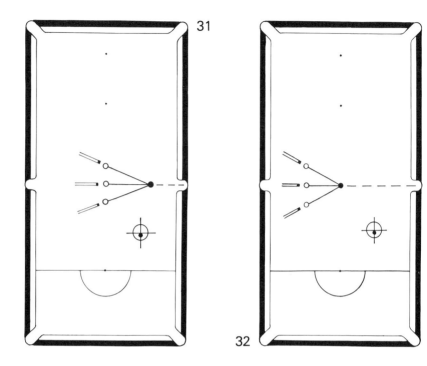

Nobody can actually teach you how to pot. But what I can do is to guide you into the easiest, quickest and most interesting ways in which you can teach yourself.

Potting balls is the art of reading angles and memorising them so that you can recognise them when they come up again. The greatest assets in this are natural ability, a powerful concentration and confidence in yourself.

In the diagrams to follow, become familiar with all the angles therein—straight shots, three-quarter ball, half-ball, quarter-ball and all the various thin ball cuts. Play them from both sides of the table into the various pockets, remember the angles and master each one, until you are able to say immediately on sight—that's a half-ball shot, and so on.

Figure 31 shows the cue-ball (white) in three positions with the object-ball (red) a foot from the centre pocket. Play the pot nice and slow and when you are sure that you can do this, replace the balls and play the same shot more firmly. Then reverse the pots to the opposite centre pocket and repeat.

Figure 32 shows a similar position, but a little more difficult, because the red ball upon the centre spot is now a greater distance from the pocket. Again play the various pots into the centre pockets from both sides of the table.

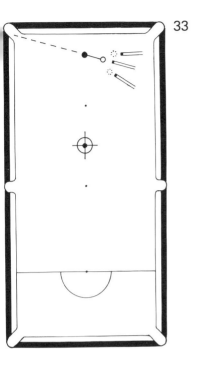

33

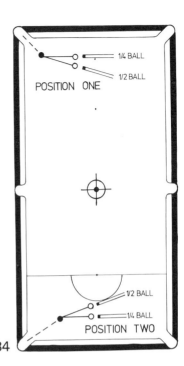

POSITION ONE

1/4 BALL
1/2 BALL

1/2 BALL
1/4 BALL

POSITION TWO

34

Do not become dejected if at first you are unable to pot the balls in figures 31 and 32. When a pot is missed replace the balls in the position and play again, only this time remember where you struck the object-ball last time and correct the angle. Be patient; do not become over confident; take your time; and concentrate. You will soon find that your percentage of successful pots will become much higher.

In figure 33 we move to the top of the table and begin playing pots from the black spots. This is a little harder because the approach to the pocket is not as open as from the centre spot.

Play nice and slow, at first gently rolling the ball into the corner pocket. Again, play into the corner pocket from both sides. When you can do this, place the cue-ball as can be seen in the dotted outlines and play from there. If you are having difficulty in potting off the black spot, then play the same pots from nearer the corner pockets, as shown in figure 33. This will help considerably in reading the angle. When this is done, keep playing this pot, but each time moving away from the pocket until you are back on the black spot.

Figure 34. Although position 1 is nice and easy, it is of great help, because the half-ball and quarter-ball pot is being played. It would be the same contact if the ball on and the cue-ball were at a greater distance from the pocket, as shown in the baulk part of the table (position 2).

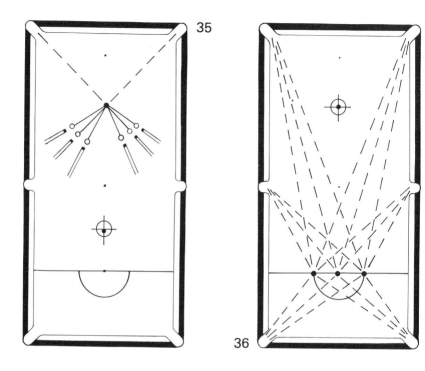

35

36

Always repeat the same shot from the opposite side of the table.

Figure 35 shows how you can build up your mastery of potting the pink from its spot at various angles into the corner pocket. It is important to be equally confident and proficient from both sides because you may be using side unintentionally. While you may subconsciously adjust to this from one side, and thus pot balls consistently, it is likely to catch you out when potting from the other side.

In figures 36 and 37 we see that the coloured balls, yellow, brown, green, blue and pink are pottable in the six pockets of the table. Although this is a little advanced, it is good to have played these various strokes to realise the possibilities of these colours. Sometimes the black is also pottable into the six pockets. As a practice exercise, place the cue-ball anywhere near each of the colours in turn and then play to pot each colour in all six pockets.

After practising these individual pots, the next move I suggest is to put all fifteen reds on the table haphazardly but all well away from the cushions. Don't put any colours on the table. Place the cue-ball anywhere you like in order to pot a red and then pot as many as you can in succession. To start with you will find that two or three is your limit but soon you will progress to 'breaks' of five, six and more. Make the practice competitive if you like and compete against a friend, scoring one for each

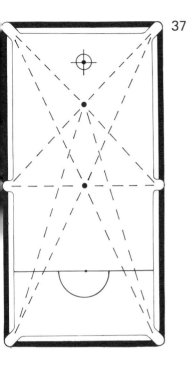

red, the highest score when all reds are potted to determine the winner.

Don't bother about positional play immediately, although it will probably begin to develop subconsciously. You will find yourself thinking 'Ah, if I take this one, I'll be able to take that one next.' Albeit in more sophisticated form, this is what positional play essentially is.

When you have become reasonably proficient at this exercise, go a stage further and place the colours on their spots with the cue-ball lined up in any position you choose for the yellow. Try to take the colours in order, yellow, green, brown, blue, pink and black, but don't be too disappointed if you find it difficult to get much beyond the green or brown.

This is where the main technique of positional play, screw and stun, come in. Indeed, without a fair command of these skills, a player's hopes of progress must be severely restricted.

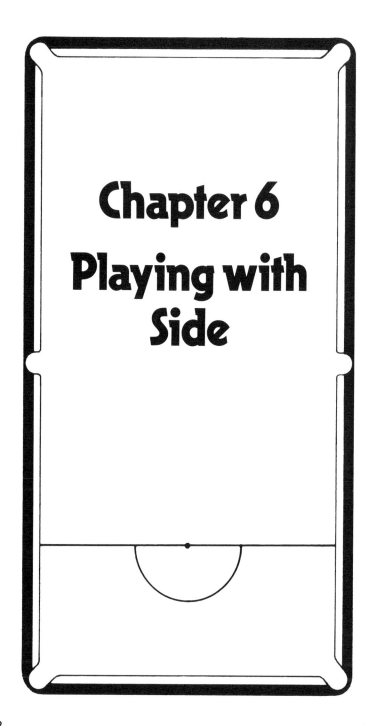

Chapter 6
Playing with Side

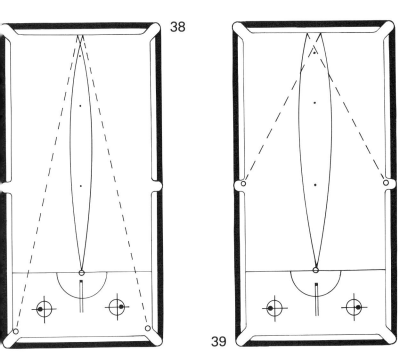

38

39

As I have said, never let practice become boring. But, having said that, some people are more easily bored than others. Indeed, there are some people who have the ability to practise systematically on their own as if they were learning a musical instrument. When this coincides with a good amount of natural talent you have the makings of a class player as systematic practice will always hasten the natural rate of improvement.

When you have mastered plain ball striking, experiment with striking the cue-ball to the left or right of centre. Place the cue-ball on the brown spot as if you were going to shoot over the spots. Then, to use right-hand side, move your bridge very slightly to the right so that your tip is still going through the cue-ball in a straight line towards the top cushion. It is most important that the cue follows this straight line rather than hitting obliquely (ie across the ball), which will affect the accuracy considerably since this produces a slight swerve effect.

The importance of this will show later when you have to pot balls with side because you will find it almost impossible if you are not hitting straight. Figure 29 has already shown that when right-hand side is used, the cue-ball first pushes out to the left, continues almost straight and then, towards the end of its journey curls to the right. The first three diagrams in this chapter also show this curve, necessarily exaggerated here to make the point in diagrammatic form. In potting with side, the

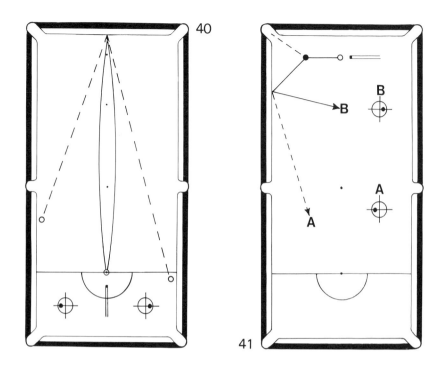

40

41

trick is to contact the ball you are trying to pot when the cue-ball is travelling more or less straight. When you hit obliquely across the ball the curl of the cue-ball is much more pronounced and therefore more difficult to gauge precisely.

For the meantime, though, start finding out the different degrees of side. Figure 38 shows two reds over the baulk pocket. Play over the spots with right-hand and left-hand side in turn, and see how near you get to potting the reds.

When you have done this, go on to the position shown in figure 39 in which the two reds are on the lips of the two middle pockets. More extreme side is needed for these strokes and novices may even find themselves miscuing.

This is the time to remind you to chalk your cue each time you play with screw or side. Also be sure to make a smooth firm stroke at the cue-ball when using side, as a sudden jerk is usually disastrous.

Other exercises in using side are easy enough to devise. Try placing reds at various points of the side cushion (figure 40) and, again shooting up the table over the spots, try to hit them on the way back as if you were escaping from snookers.

Now, having outlined the basics of side, is the time to introduce a note of caution. *Never* use side unless you have to as it always makes the pot

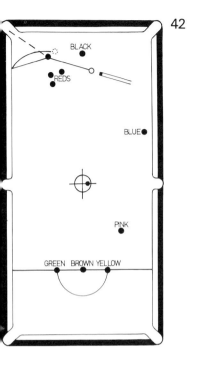

42

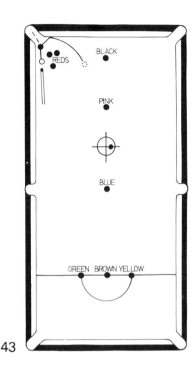

43

more difficult than it would be without. Take no notice of those characters who astound their friends by the amount (rather than the effectiveness) of the side they use. 'Did you see that?' someone will say, wide-eyed, as the cue-ball comes off a cushion at a wide angle. 'The side that Old Harry had on that ball was amazing. It just zipped off the cushion. I've never seen anything like it.' Of course, the fact that Old Harry didn't *need* all that side, or that the amount of side was unintentional, is often forgotten; an effect has been created and Harry is the hero.

Remember that side is useless unless it is controlled. Never, never, never address the centre of the cue-ball and then apply side. And do not be deluded into thinking that striking on the extreme edge of the ball will cause more side to be applied. The only thing that is likely to be applied in this case is a miscue.

As you become more expert, try to incorporate into your stroke a slightly sharper impact of the cue-tip on the cue-ball. This will not be necessary when cue-ball and object-ball are close together because the spin will not have had time to evaporate, but in situations when they are further apart I have come to regard this sharp impact striking as an important part of my game. The trick is to stop it becoming a jab. Only your sense of touch will enable you to distinguish between the two.

There are two types of side: running and check. Running side makes the cue-ball take a wider angle and makes the cue-ball accelerate; check side makes the cue-ball take a narrower angle and decelerate. Figure 41 shows the simple pot being played first with running (left-hand) side (shot A) and then with (right-hand) check side (shot B).

Taken in isolation like this, the use of side is pointless but it becomes relevant when you want to manoeuvre the cue-ball into a particular position for your next shot. For instance, figure 42 shows an easy pot red but a plain ball pot will mean that the cue-ball will bounce off the cushion into the reds and no doubt leave you snookered on the black. However, if you play with check (right-hand) side, as you did in shot B, figure 41 the cue-ball will miss the reds and leave you on the black.

This is only half the story—at least to an experienced player—for the angle at which the cue-ball is left to pot the black means that the cue-ball will naturally move into a good position for the next red, either by bouncing off the cushion or by means of a screw shot—but more of that later.

Figure 43 shows another simple position, this time using running side. Again the problem is that a plain ball shot will take the cue-ball slap into some of the other reds but a little right-hand (running) side will take the cue-ball round them nicely to leave perfect position.

A word of warning: remember that running side increases the speed of the cue-ball both off the cushion and, to a limited extent, along the cloth itself. So play this shot slightly slower than you would if you were playing without side, as the cue-ball will otherwise run too far to leave a comfortable pot on the black.

Chapter 7

Stop, Stun and Screw Shots

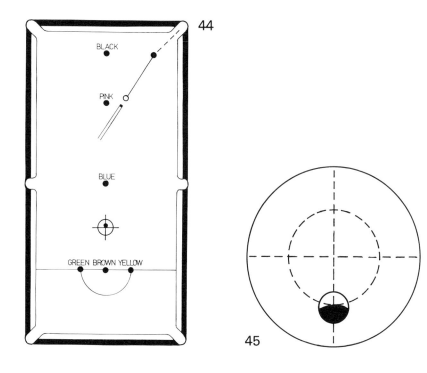

44

45

It is no accident that the pots with side I have described in the previous chapter are all very easy in that the object-ball is near a pocket and the cue-ball is near the object-ball. Even good players are wary about using side for more difficult shots if there is any reasonable alternative, and you will find the 'stop', 'stun' and 'screw' shots I am going to deal with in this chapter will be the more faithful friends in the long run.

Stop Shots

To start with the 'stop' shots, which is another name for a straight stun pot: in figure 44 you have a straight red into the top pocket. Beginners tend to roll these shots in but this is a bad habit for several reasons. First, if you play at just the strength for the red to reach the pocket, it will remain in the jaw as a sitter for your opponent should you happen to miss. Played more briskly on the other hand, the red may well finish safe if you fail to pot it.

This, of course, is an easy shot and you should attempt it with 100 per cent confidence, but there will be other more difficult shots where the chances of success may be 75–25, 50–50 or even less. In fact, the longer the odds against a successful pot, the more thought you should give to what is likely to happen if you miss.

Perhaps an even more important reason for not rolling your pots is that

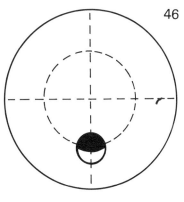

46

comparatively few tables run absolutely true. The cue-ball may 'run off' before it contacts the object-ball and the object-ball may run off as it travels towards the pocket. Either way, it is better to play with medium strength when you can.

Coming back to figure 44, the need for a 'stop' shot is obvious because otherwise the cue-ball, from a plain ball medium-paced shot, will simply follow through near or even into the pocket.

Figure 45 shows where the tip should contact the cue-ball in order to stop the ball dead if cue-ball and object-ball are not more than three feet apart. However, you will need to strike lower to achieve the same effect if cue-ball and object-ball are more than three feet apart (see figure 46). Remember that, if you want to stop the ball dead, the cue-ball must be carrying some backspin at the moment of impact. The further away the object-ball is, the more backspin you will need to apply in order to prevent the backspin evaporating before contacting the object-ball. This is achieved by striking lower and in certain cases harder.

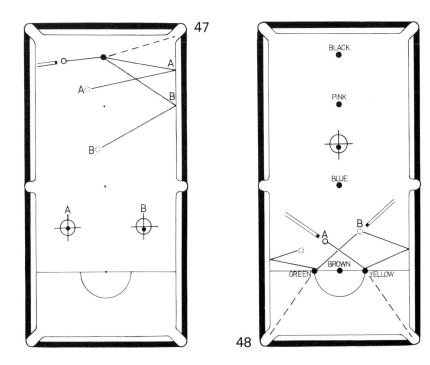

47

48

Stun Shots

When the pot is not straight, the 'stop' shot becomes a stun. As the term implies, stun 'kills' the cue-ball's normal forward movement. In figure 47, line A shows the natural half-ball angle from a plain ball shot while line B shows the wider angle if stun is used. The value of this is obvious if we refer to clearing the colours in sequence.

It is possible to clear the colours using only plain ball shots but if you restrict yourself in this way it is fatally easy to get into a hopeless tangle. For example, in figure 48, the yellow could be potted plain ball but this would then leave the cue-ball with a thin pot on the green and more difficulty brewing ahead in getting good position on the brown. By playing a stun on the yellow, however, the cue-ball will finish at a similar angle to pot the green.

Figure 49 shows that, after potting the green, there is a nice angle to pot the brown with stun and finish on the blue. Roll in the blue (this is an easy shot because, with cue-ball and object-ball not far apart, you can afford to do this) and leave a three-quarter ball pot on the pink. This stun is again the shot to play, leaving an easy black to complete your clearance.

66

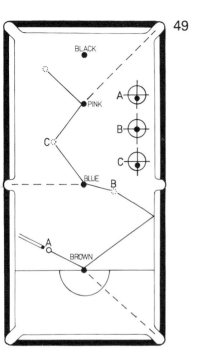

Screw Shots

With your stop and stun strokes to add to your plain ball shots you are now starting to build up a repertoire of skills. But what if, in potting the yellow, the cue-ball finishes straight on the green? The plain ball pot will leave only an awkward pot into the middle pocket with no prospect of gaining good position on the blue while the stop shot will leave you only a thin cut on the brown, easily missed, with uncertain position to follow.

For this situation, you need to acquire a screw shot.

Screw is the Snooker term for backspin. It is imparted by the tip striking the cue-ball below centre so that it is skidding backwards as it travels towards the object-ball. When contact is made with the object-ball, the backspin becomes operative and the cue-ball springs back.

The amount of screw or backspin which it is possible to generate in a given situation is dependent on four factors: 1 the distance between cue-ball and object ball; 2 the amount of power used in the stroke; 3 the depth at which the cue-tip contacts the cue-ball; and 4 the condition of the cloth.

The distance between the cue-ball and object-ball is relevant because spin gradually evaporates. Thus, the greater the distance, the more difficult it is to impart enough spin to 'hold' the ball.

Power is needed either to shorten the time taken between cue-ball

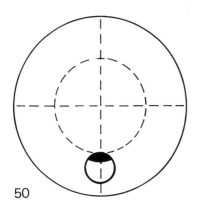

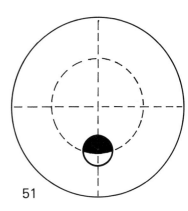

50   51

and object-ball (thus leaving less time for the spin to evaporate) or to make the cue-ball rebound from object-ball with greater force, thus increasing the distance of the screw back.

The precise point at which the tip strikes the cue-ball is relevant for although it may be possible to screw back slightly hitting only just below centre if cue-ball and object-ball are close together, a much lower tip contact will have to be made if the balls are further apart. This needs careful judgement. Strike too low (figure 50) and a miscue results. Strike slightly higher (figure 51) so that there is maximum contact between tip and ball (see shaded areas again) and you should have no problems. Try this initially by placing the blue on its spot and the cue-ball some nine inches from it in a straight line.

Confidence is the most important element in playing this shot satisfactorily. You must try from the start to put out of your mind any notion that there is anything special about a screw shot. Many players go wrong before they even hit the cue-ball. They think: 'Right, screw shot, special effort required.' Their grip tightens on the cue, they address the cue-ball with a long sweeping backswing as if they are going to hit it at 1,000 mph, and point the cue-tip so low at the cue-ball that if it actually hit it there it would take a couple of inches out of the cloth and spoon the ball into the front row of the stalls!

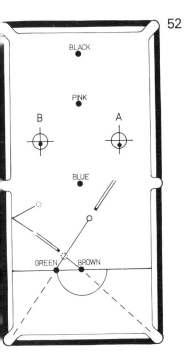

52

Novices might well remember the following points in the hope that they will assimilate them so thoroughly that they will soon require no conscious thought to incorporate into their games.

1 Lower or tilt the bridge slightly and lower the back arm to ensure that the cue is still driving into the cue-ball horizontally. This will allow your domed tip maximum grip on the round surface of the ball.

2 Keep the muscles in your cue-arm relaxed. A smooth action and follow through are essential to good screw shots and these cannot be achieved if your arm muscles are tense.

3 Make sure your tip strikes where you think you are aiming. The natural tendency for novices is for the tip to strike higher than they intend, perhaps out of a subconscious fear of miscuing.

4 Make sure the cue strikes the cue-ball firmly with a full stroke. Don't stab at it nervously.

Very soon you will find the cue-ball springing back quite easily and you will develop the 'touch' to control the precise distance the cue-ball recoils. This will become important later in game situations for it is more use to be able to screw back nine inches accurately than nine feet if you are trying for six feet.

Thus, returning again to the problem of clearing the colours, play to pot the green and screw back about four inches (figure 52) to leave a half-ball

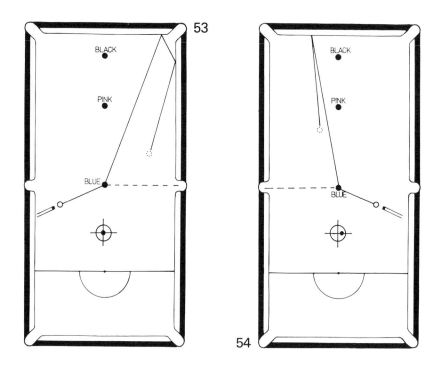

or three-quarter ball pot on the brown as this, in turn, will leave a simple stun pot taking the cue-ball off the side cushion for the blue.

The importance of screwing back accurately over a short distance is revealed by figure 52, shot 2, since this assumes that the cue-ball has recoiled further than intended so that it has finished straight on the next ball, the brown. All is not lost since position on the blue can still be obtained by a so-called deep screw bringing the cue-ball back to the side cushion and off it, as shown. But it is undoubtedly more difficult than if you had controlled the screw off the green perfectly and left the simple half-ball stun using the side cushion. It requires more power and thus more controlled cueing. The cue-ball may drop short and leave an awkward cut blue into the middle or it may finish right on the side cushion, a shot which not even a professional likes.

This simple example shows that the object of the exercise is to try to construct your breaks in such a way that you have a series of easy shots.

Viewers of 'Pot Black' constantly ask me how many shots I think ahead, expecting me to say six or seven or even more. In fact, I generally think two ahead though later possible developments in the break may be in the back of my mind at the same time. Thus, in the present instance, I would be thinking two shots ahead by not only leaving myself in a position to pot the brown (one) but leaving myself in a position where, with maximum ease, I can pot it to get on the blue (two).

The key stages of clearing the colours are getting from brown to blue and from blue to pink. For instance, anything less than perfect position of the blue may lead to using one or two cushions, as in figures 53 and 54 to get on to the pink.

With this type of shot, half the battle is recognising the angle at which the cue-ball leaves the object-ball; indeed, in distinguishing between the angle which will take the cue-ball on and off the cushion and the angle which will take the cue-ball into a pocket. Equally, it is undesirable to pot the blue in such a way that the cue-ball finishes under the side cushion. Therefore, in figure 54 you need right-hand side to check the cue-ball off the top cushion to leave perfect position on the pink.

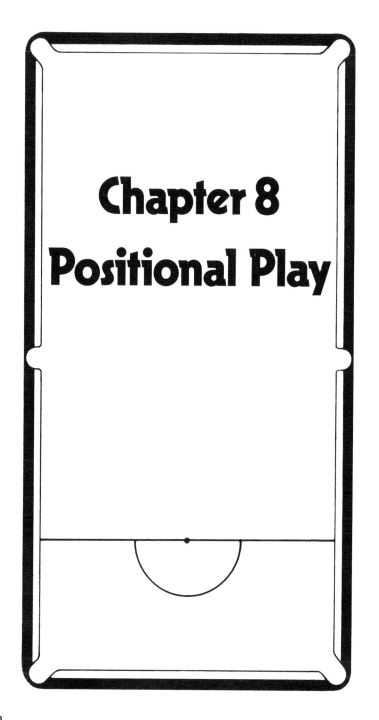

Chapter 8
Positional Play

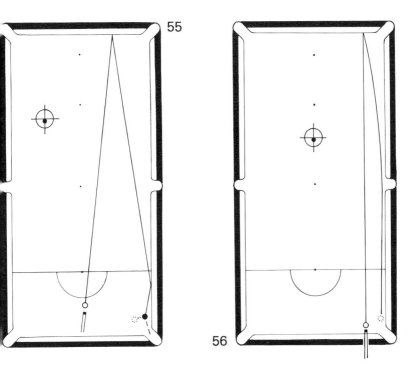

55

56

Having learned the basics of straightforward potting and grasped some idea of the main positional techniques of screw, side and stun, it is time to consider the art of positional play.

Most players, through lack of thought, find that after potting a red they are not on a colour either because the stroke was not played strongly enough, or was played too strongly, or because there was no colour on at all. Therefore, think before potting a red and study the layout of the table to see where you require the cue-ball to be after potting the red.

Always remember that the most important ball on the table is the cue-ball. In other words, I am telling you to master the cue-ball and make it do what you want it to. Screw, stun and side are important but the most fundamental arts of all are control of strength and knowledge of angles.

Learn the feel of applying various strengths to the cue-ball. The quickest and easiest way is to play the cue-ball up the table from the baulk line and return it to within two inches of the baulk cushion. Play this and use as many variations as you can.

In my early days my favourite way of practising to read and learn angles was to place a ball near a corner pocket and, treating it as a snooker, trying to pot the ball. At the same time, to develop your judgement of strength, make sure that you move the object-ball only a little.

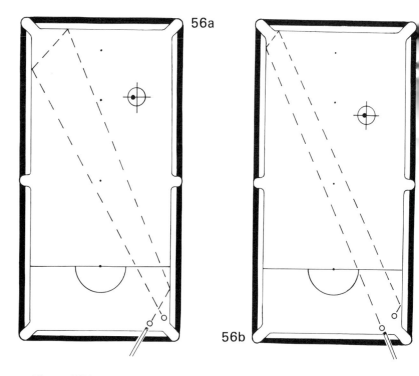

56a

56b

Figure 55 is a simple straightforward plain ball stroke, pushing the red nearer the pocket or even into it. From the position in which the balls stop or from a similar position, play the cue-ball up the table again, as in figure 56, and keep repeating. As you do so, experiment with a variety of cushion angles. Figure 56a shows how the position in figure 56 can be approached with a three-cushion shot instead of the simple one-cushion shot. Figure 56b shows yet another variation, this time using left-hand side as check. Another good exercise is illustrated in figure 57 which makes use of the side cushion. This is more difficult but will help you to further your knowledge of angles. For instance, although A and C **are** in fact the same they look different.

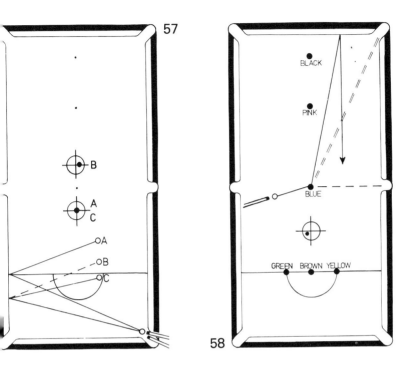

57

58

The Four Principles

It could be argued that there are four kinds of positional play: 1 avoiding
an in-off; 2 avoiding finishing under a cushion; 3 obtaining the best
possible position to pot the next ball; 4 obtaining the best position in
relation to potting a series of balls.

It might be as well at this stage to take a quick refresher course on
some of the common in-offs which Snooker players the world over fall for
time after time.

Figure 58 is a natural angle for an in-off in the corner as you pot the
blue in the middle. The in-off is avoided and position on the pink obtained
by potting the blue with stun and left-hand side.

The pot black in the corner pocket in figure 59 is also a natural in-off in
the middle. It is avoided by using screw and, if the striker finds it easier
this way, a little right-hand side. As the contact with the object-ball is a
thin one it requires some touch and experience to make the cue-ball 'bite'
on such a small part of the object-ball. The tendency for beginners, in
trying to make sure of screwing enough to miss the middle pocket, is to
hit the object-ball too thick and miss the pot.

Figure 60 shows a recurrent in-off in the middle pocket in potting a ball
into the top. Right-hand (check) side or left-hand (running) side are
generally the best ways of avoiding the in-off but in certain circum-

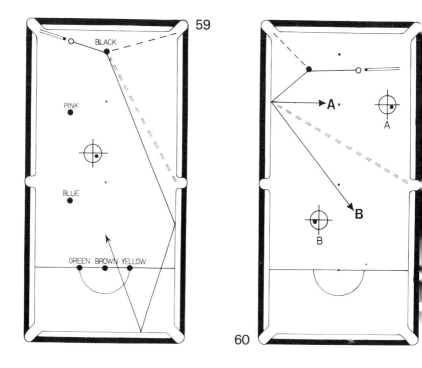

BLACK

PINK

BLUE

GREEN BROWN YELLOW

A

A

B

B

stances (usually for positional reasons) the screw even off the thin contact may be used.

Figure 61 shows a natural in-off in the corner as a consequence of a natural pot into the middle. Play here with screw and right-hand side. The latter will help you keep the cue-ball away from a cushion for your next shot.

Figure 62 illustrates how the middle pockets always seem bigger for the cue-ball than the object-ball! If you tried to pot a ball along the dotted line drawn from the top cushion to the middle pocket, the shot would look quite awkward. Play the pot shown in this diagram and it is amazing how often the cue-ball will bounce off the top cushion and go in the middle pocket as clean as a whistle. Avoid it by using screw and left-hand side or both.

Left-hand side is the best way of avoiding the baulk pocket in-off when playing safety shots from the main pack of reds to bring the cue-ball back to the baulk cushion (figure 63).

Figure 64 shows a common three cushion in-off. Again, avoid it by playing with left-hand side.

Figure 65 illustrates a type of shot which can crop up at any stage of a frame but most often seems to materialise at the end. With only a thin cut black to win, many a player has had the elation of potting it only for it to

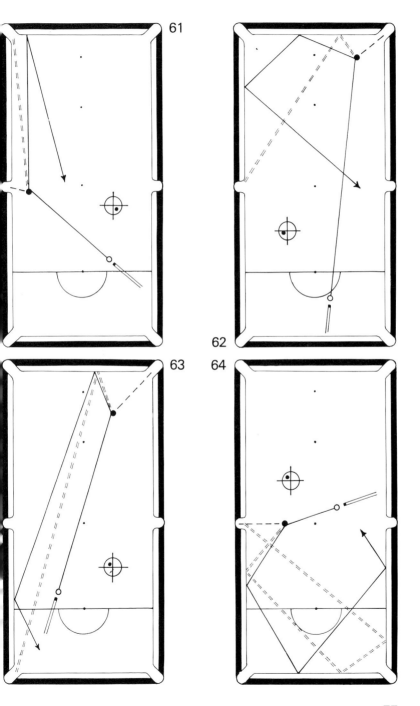

61

62

63   64

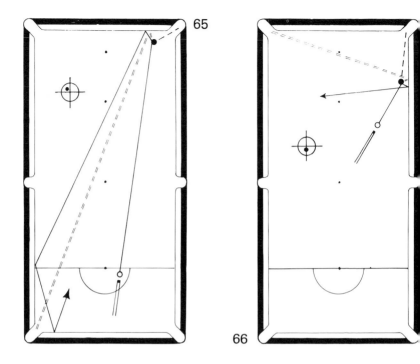

66

give way to disappointment as the cue-ball flies in-off into the baulk pocket. Never be tempted to play a pot at this distance slowly. Use a little left-hand side and all should be well. Use too much and the cue-ball could rebound off three cushions and finish in the middle pocket.

The position in figure 66 has often given a similar disappointment. The black is not too easy and many players have concentrated so hard on potting it that they have forgotten that a natural plain ball pot will take the cue-ball into the opposite corner pocket. Play the shot firmly with screw or stun to avoid this but don't use side because this will only make the pot more difficult.

Avoiding finishing under a cushion is often just a matter of controlling the speed of the cue-ball. Figure 67 shows a very easy red into the middle pocket which even novices take with the firm idea of potting the blue next. It is obvious that, at whatever strength the red is potted, there will be an almost straight blue to follow. Accordingly, novices tend to roll the pot in and leave the cue-ball either on or near the cushion.

It is easy enough for good players to miss simple-looking shots if they either have to point the cue downwards at the cue-ball or cue awkwardly at the top of the cue-ball with two-thirds of it buried under the cushion, so they always take pains to leave position not just for a possible pot, nor just for an easy pot, but for a pot so easy that they can give almost all their

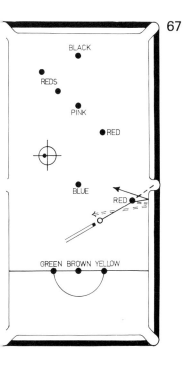

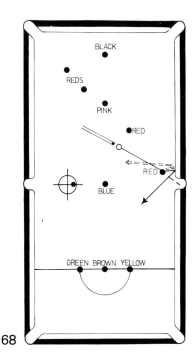

attention to positioning the cue-ball and very little to the easy pot itself.

Therefore, this particular almost straight pot can either be played as a stun to leave the cue-ball nearly where the red was but at a slightly wider angle on the blue, or, as I would prefer in this case, to bounce off the cushion for a slightly straighter angle on the blue which would enable you to get position easily on one of the other reds in potting the blue.

This very simple shot also illustrates the sound general principle that it is better for the cue-ball to come towards the ball on which you are playing position rather than go away from it. In other words, it is usually better, if you have a choice, for the cue-ball to bounce off the cushion towards the next ball rather than be rolling towards the cushion away from the next ball. By coming 'into' the shot, each inch (within reason) is improving your position; by going 'away' from the shot, each inch is making it more difficult.

Figure 68 is slightly more advanced than 67 because novices can again see that they only have to tap the red into the middle pocket to have an easy blue to follow. However, if you play this pot with no side the cue-ball will finish on what every good player will call the 'wrong' side of the blue. In other words, in potting the blue, the cue-ball will be travelling further away from the remaining reds. Therefore, play the pot with strong right-hand side to take the cue-ball the other side of the blue, leaving it

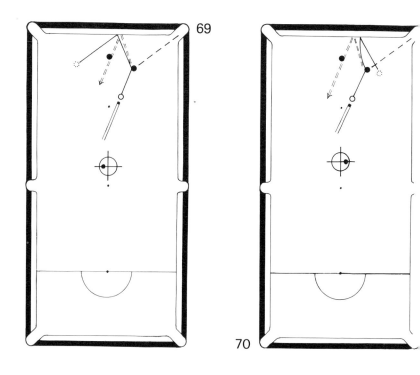

just as easy to pot but, more important, with good position on your next red a hundred times easier to obtain.

These very simple examples have illustrated the four principles of positional play which I set out earlier: you have avoided an in-off; you have avoided finishing under a cushion; you have obtained the best possible position to pot the next ball; and you have the best position in relation to potting a series of balls.

On the other hand, there are times when two or more of these principles may be in conflict. It can sometimes pay to leave a position rather more difficult than it need be in order to give yourself a better chance of obtaining the longer term consideration of getting a more advantageous position later in the break.

As your knowledge of angles develops you ought to find yourself using side and screw for more complex positional reasons. For instance, in figure 69, a plain half-ball pot on the red will mean that the cue-ball will bounce off the cushion and hit the black, thus making it difficult to continue your break. However, by playing the pot with a little left-hand (running) side, the cue-ball will take a wider angle from the top cushion and come round the black to leave perfect position. Alternatively, play this pot with right-hand (check) side so that the cue-ball spins the other way off the top cushion to leave the black in the opposite top pocket (figure 70).

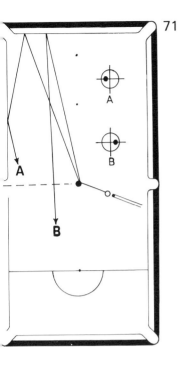

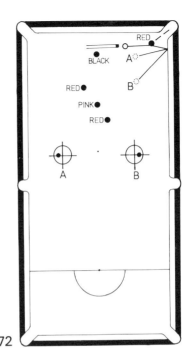

Unless the position of other balls points clearly to one of these alternatives as the better, the use of running or check side is a matter of personal preference. John Spencer tends to prefer running side and Alex Higgins check. I don't mind particularly, but usually use running side if the table is slow and check if it is fast.

Another situation in which either check or running side can be used is in figure 71, when there is often a choice between quarter-ball cut on the blue using left-hand side and two cushions or right-hand side and one cushion. Master both so that, depending upon the precise position of any other balls, you can employ either.

As you play more and more, certain general points about positional play will start to emerge. It will become obvious that the black plays a most important role in break building and that to give yourself maximum scope for manoeuvre it is usually desirable to leave yourself a half-ball or three-quarter ball angle on the black so that you can obtain position on your next red.

Briefly, the object of positional play is to leave yourself a series of easy shots, as in figure 72, when your first shot is an easy red over the top pocket. Most novices will trickle the red in and be so glad to be able to pot the black as well that they will plan no further. This is where a little thought will pay dividends and where you will quickly appreciate the

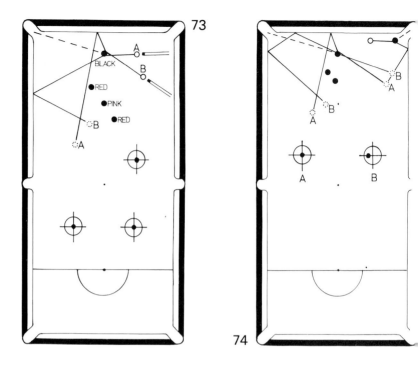

dangers of leaving yourself a straight black without considering what comes next. If you do this in figure 72, all you can do is screw back a little to leave an awkward red into a middle pocket, so use a little left-hand (check) side (shot A) or a little right-hand (running) side (shot B) so that you can use either the top or the side cushion (figure 73, B) or, the shot would play, the stun (figure 73, A).

Of course, if the position is different (figure 74), you must make sure you pot the easy initial red in such a way that you can either use the top or the top and side cushions, as shown, for position on either of the two reds by the black spot.

Figure 74 is a straightforward position but it immediately highlights two invaluable strokes which recur again and again. It is generally helpful for instance, to play the top and side cushion stroke with top and left-hand side thus giving the cue-ball an extra zip off the cushion and cutting down the actual cue-power you will need.

As you play more, gradually accustom yourself to potting the black with screw, side and stun at all angles because this is an area of the game which is vital for any ambitious player.

One of the ways in which I can generally spot that someone is primarily a Billiards player who has later progressed to Snooker is his greater readiness to use the cushion rather than a more direct route. In

82

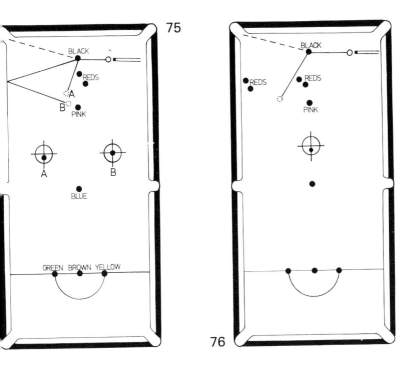

75

76

figure 75, position on the red can be obtained either by potting the black and coming off the cushion (shot A) or by stunning in the black and gaining the position direct (shot B). The snag about using the cushions when you don't have to is that you have to gauge the speed both of the cushions and the bed of the table. There is also the point that another ball may be in the way, as in figure 76 where you have no choice but to play the stun.

When you start making bigger breaks you will find that congestion is often the big problem in compiling a break and that a considerable degree of skill and control will be needed to prevent the cue-ball cannoning into other balls and ruining your position.

However, never put your control under more pressure than you need to. In figure 77, for instance, don't be so obsessed with the black that you forget about all the other colours on the table. You are attempting quite an awkward quarter-ball red and you need some left-hand side to avoid cannoning into the pink. Don't try and hold position on what would in any event be an awkward black but play the shot with a shade more strength so that you can take the simple blue next—an easy position from which you can then plan how to continue your break.

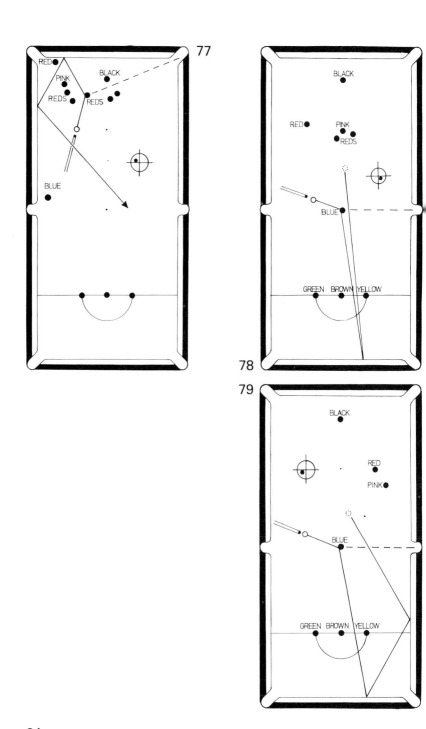

77

78

79

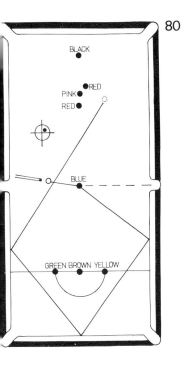

Recovery Play

Try as you might to perfect one's positional play, there will be many times when ideal position is lost and it becomes necessary to play a recovery shot to keep the break going. This may not necessarily take the form of a specially good pot. It may be that your next pot is still easy enough though not at the angle you wanted it to obtain good position on the next ball.

A recurring example of this is getting on the 'wrong' side of the blue. Figures 78–81 show four common methods of regaining good position when this happens. All require good control since the cue-ball has to avoid kissing any of the small value colours.

Figure 78 shows the cue-ball going between yellow and brown and back on virtually the same line. This is done by using stun and right-hand (check) side. Aim to get nearer the yellow than the brown as the cue-ball crosses the baulk line for the first time or you will tend to have the cue-ball kissing the brown on the way back.

Figure 79 is a shot which most players find more difficult than that shown in figure 78. This requires stun and running (left-hand) side, taking the cue-ball first between yellow and brown and, coming back, between yellow and side cushion.

The shot in figure 80 can be used when there is not enough angle for the stun in and out of baulk. Play it with top, right-hand side and plenty of power.

85

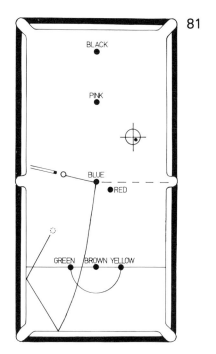

Figure 81 requires screw and right-hand side to get the cue-ball first between brown and green and then between green and side cushion. It can be used quite comfortably for a shot such as the one shown but because screw shortens the run of the cue-ball it is usually impracticable to use it when you need to get the cue-ball up near the black spot for your next shot.

Chapter 9
Safety Play

Everybody knows (or thinks he knows) that the object of safety play is to leave your opponent in a safe position, that is, a position from which he cannot score. But the real art of safety play is to leave your opponent not only safe but in such a position that he will be hard put not to give you an opening. In other words, your ideal should be an apparent paradox: attacking safety.

To begin at the beginning, the first safety shot you will play is the break-off. I have seen club players simply roll up to the reds, leaving their opponent with no chance of scoring admittedly, but equally without putting them under the slightest pressure to make an important or perhaps vital mistake. Figure 82 shows the break-off I recommend, striking the outside red with right-hand side and swinging the cue-ball off three cushions to finish on the baulk cushion behind the green. If you play this shot perfectly (and with practice you should do so quite often) you have immediately put your opponent under pressure. There will be two or three loose reds and if he is playing the length of the table from under the cushion he could bungle his answering safety shot and give you a good chance to take a useful early lead.

The early stages of most frames usually consist of an exchange of safety shots until one player leaves a ball which the other feels he has a good chance of potting and obtaining position on a colour. Most people will advise you to play this shot thin and this is good advice in certain circumstances. It is, for instance, pointless to bring the cue-ball back to the baulk cushion if you bring a red with it, which is what will happen if you hit a red half-ball and it is not impeded by another ball as it travels down the table. There will be just as much speed on that red after impact as on the cue-ball so they will return down the table together. A thin contact will mean that the cue-ball will have more speed on it after impact than the object-ball and a thicker than half-ball contact will mean that the object-ball will have more speed on it.

In practice, a thicker than half-ball contact in a safety exchange means that the cue-ball remains near the pack of reds, usually in a good position for your opponent. However, the thin safety shot to the baulk cushion has certain limitations. The chief of these to my mind is that it is often a negative form of safety play: it leaves your opponent safe but it is just as easy for him to leave you safe. These long drawn out safety battles consist of waiting for someone to play a bad shot rather than trying to force the issue. When this happens, there is a tendency for players to lose their potting rhythm and for a frame to develop untidily.

Many players keep playing thin safety shots off reds which are in or by the pack because they are afraid of disturbing the pack too much and leaving their opponent a chance to pot a long one. I try not to fall into this negative frame of mind and take the first opportunity to open the pack by contacting a red about half-ball or a little less. I do not do this recklessly. Indeed, I make a point of getting the cue-ball back as near to the baulk cushion as possible. This means that, even if a long pot is on, it

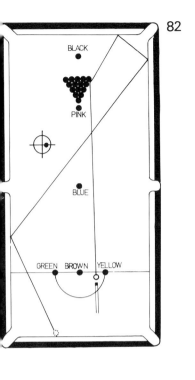

82

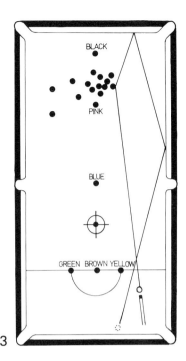

83

will require a good shot to get it. My philosophy is that my opponent will miss more than he gets and therefore, over a period, my tactics pay off.

Figures 83 and 84 show what I mean. Many players would play thinly off the end red as shown in figure 83. Such a shot is safe as houses but easy for your opponent to play safe, even if the cue-ball finishes behind one of the low value colours, in which case he would play slowly off a cushion and roll up to the pack.

Figure 84 is the shot I would probably play: just less than half-ball with right-hand side on the outside red of the pack, opening up the pack and leaving my opponent a long way away.

My method is either more positive or more risky depending on how your mind works. The safety duel has to be resolved one way or another: my aim is to resolve it quickly, believing that my chances of getting in first are better with this 'sudden death' attitude than with the wearing down tactics which some players favour.

The first couple of shots in a safety exchange are usually quite straight-forward. The triangle of reds is not very much disturbed so there are few or no awkward obstacles to bringing the cue-ball off the top cushion or top and side cushions. However, in any safety exchange you should always be looking either for a reasonable chance of a pot or an oppor-tunity not just to leave your opponent safe but to put him in trouble.

89

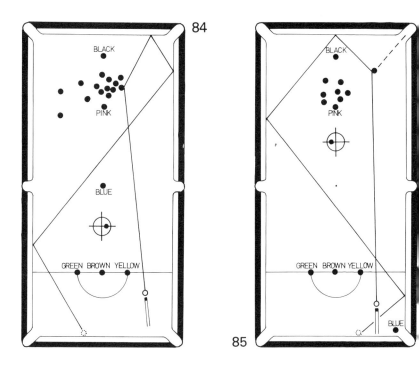

Figure 84 is an example of the latter. The straightforward thin return down the right-hand side of the table will give your opponent a chance to make a similar reply (figure 83), but if you play your safety shot thin but with strong right-hand side to swing the cue-ball off three cushions over to the left of the table it is immediately obvious that your opponent will struggle either to make an answering return to the baulk cushion or to sort out a pot. You will notice here that you have played the very best kind of safety shot, opened the reds and yet left no chance for a pot.

Another especially valuable shot in these opening exchanges is the 'shot to nothing', that is, a shot when you can attempt a pot in the knowledge that, even if you miss it, your opponent will be left in a safe position. A common example of this is shown in figure 85 where, playing with left-hand side, you can attempt the loose red into the top right-hand pocket while at the same time bringing the cue-ball off three cushions to the safety of the baulk cushion. Unless the red wobbles in the jaws of the pocket and stops over it, which is unlikely with this kind of shot, your opponent will only be able to play either a safety shot or a difficult long pot.

When, as in this diagram, one of the colours is handily placed, the blue in this case, this sort of shot is even more attractive because, if the red is potted, the blue is available as a prelude to what should be a useful break. If there is no convenient ball, like the blue in the diagram, I still play the pot but aim to drop the ball just short of the baulk line so that I can take one of the small colours and go up the table again. This is another instance where my own method of play is more adventurous than most.

Many players, including quite a few professionals, will be so afraid of missing the pot that they will take great care to bring the cue-ball right back to the baulk cushion: safe if they miss and with the chance to roll up behind a small colour for a snooker if they pot it. At a modest local level this cautious approach sometimes pays off, but I base my own game on getting the '50–50' shots or even the '40–60' shots, and attack accordingly. In short, I try to win primarily through my own strengths rather than from trying to squeeze mistakes out of my opponent.

Be positive, but don't be reckless. Be brave, but don't be stupid. If you need to take a risk, take it boldly, but if you can attack without taking a risk then, of course, it stands to reason, that is better.

Therefore, in a safety exchange, apply sound business principles: what shot offers the most potential at the least risk or, sometimes, how to make your opponent take the greatest risk for the least potential profit.

Shots to nothing often play an important part in tight competitive snooker but it is always best to approach them with a positive attitude. Many players regard the safety part of the stroke as the most important and only play the pot half-heartedly. Look upon the stroke instead as a chance to take the initiative rather than just to contain your opponent.

By no means all shots to nothing are as obvious as the one in figure 84. You will see professionals constantly studying the precise lie of the balls before they play to see if a red can just squeeze between a number of surrounding reds into one of the top pockets (like figure 86 for instance).

Even when the reds are still bunched together, a shot to nothing may be on by way of a plant or set. I will return to these useful shots more fully later, but just for now figure 87 shows two reds touching in such a way that any glancing blow on the first red from the cue-ball is bound to send the second ball into the pocket.

Figures 88 and 89 show two more useful methods of returning the cue-ball to the baulk cushion. In figure 88 left-hand (running) side is necessary to swing the cue-ball round behind the black to avoid kissing either the black or another red.

Figure 89 can have serious consequences if the shot goes wrong—as it may well if you are not cueing accurately. The idea of the shot is to play thin off the red with left-hand side so that the cue-ball avoids kissing the other reds and spins off top and side cushions (it will gather speed after leaving the side cushion as the check side from the top cushion becomes running side as it hits the side cushion) before finishing, you hope, on or near the baulk cushion.

It is important to contact the red thinly, for a half-ball contact will mean that the cue-ball and red will kiss as the red rebounds from the side cushion, thus leaving the cue-ball in the top part of the table and probably in a good position for your opponent.

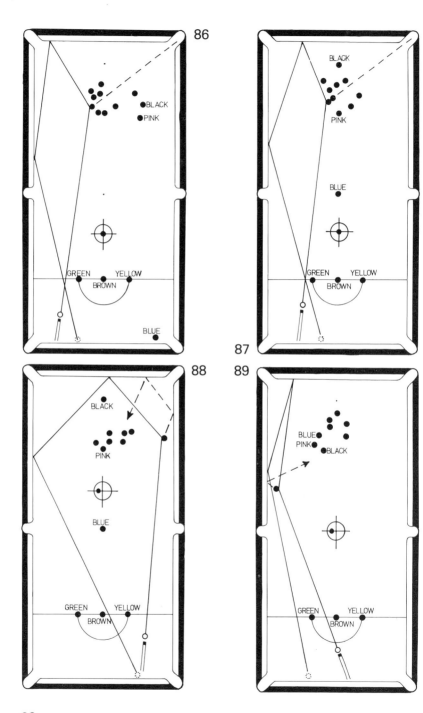

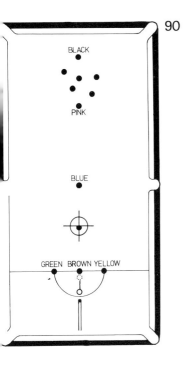

Safety Play—Middle Game

Whereas the opening exchanges of a frame follow a fairly standard pattern because it takes time for the initial set up of the table, particularly the triangle of reds, to be well and truly disturbed, the middle part of a frame may see the balls in an infinite number of different positions. Therefore in the middle of a frame you have to be tactically more alert, for it is unlikely that either you or your opponent has a decisive lead.

It is in the middle of a frame that the snooker often comes into its own as a tactical weapon. Except towards the end of a frame, when the total value of the balls remaining is less than the points difference between the two players, the snooker is more valuable in forcing your opponent into an error than in extracting penalty points. No one has ever won a frame entirely through snookering and penalty points so always remember that in the end you have to pot balls to win.

Figure 90 shows the simplest, yet one of the most valuable, snookers you can play. You have just potted a red and have a choice of the three baulk colours. Both the yellow and green are at the wrong angle for a pot to take the cue-ball up the table for the remaining reds, and the brown is either an awkward cut into the middle pocket or an equally risky long one into the top. The only shot here is the 'dirty' snooker, or roll up on the brown.

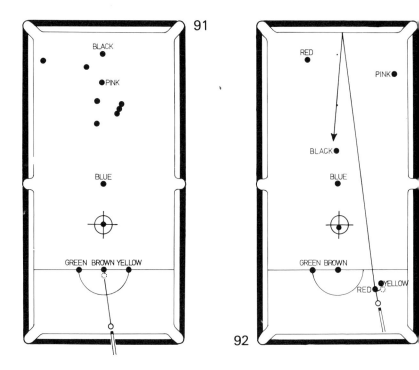

This seems so easy and obvious that it may hardly seem worth a diagram, but look more closely and observe that the brown has moved only a fraction of an inch from its spot and the cue-ball is nestling almost against it.

Many players appear to think that as long as they have left a snooker they have played a good shot. The better player will concentrate on making the snooker as difficult as he possibly can so that, as the diagram shows, he leaves the cue-ball so near the brown that the straightforward one-cushion escape off the side cushion is blocked.

In figure 91 it is much more difficult to do this. From six inches away it is quite simple to roll on to the brown at exactly dead weight but it is dangerous to attempt to do so from a distance of about two feet. If you drop an inch or two short of the brown you have given four points away and, worse, you will then have to play the nasty escape which you tried to inflict on your opponent.

This is, therefore, one of those times when it is better to be a shade too hard than a shade too soft and it is unrealistic, particularly in a tense match, to attempt a weight of shot so precise that you deny your opponent the escape off the side cushion. It is much more positive to leave a snooker with the object-ball or balls in the open rather than under or near a cushion.

94

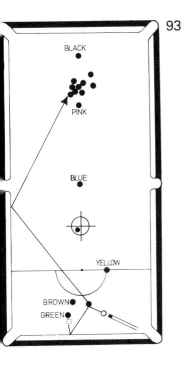

Figure 92 shows what I mean. It is child's play to push the red a few inches and roll behind the yellow but much more constructive to stun the red so that it travels well up the table, well away from the cushion. This not only makes the éscape difficult but much more dangerous for your opponent because both reds are pottable instead of just one.

Figure 93 shows another example of putting your opponent under maximum pressure from a snooker, screwing off the red behind the brown and sending the red off two cushions to split the cluster of reds near the black spot. Use a little left-hand side with the screw for this shot to check the cue-ball as it comes off the baulk cushion.

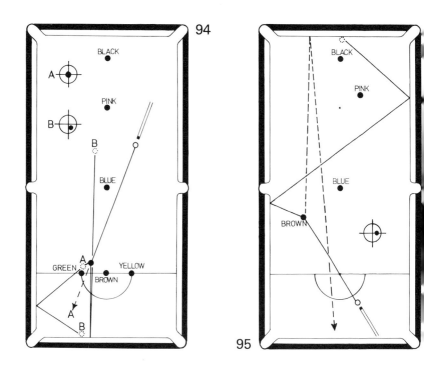

Safety Play—End Game

Towards the end of a frame, snookering may still be primarily tactical though there are occasions when you will need snookers plus all the remaining balls to win.

The most important rule to remember when attempting to lay a snooker is never to push the object-ball near a pocket unless you are absolutely certain of laying the snooker successfully—and usually not even then. The obvious reason for this is that if you leave your opponent a clear sight of a ball near a pocket he will probably pot it and remove any slender hope you had of recovering to win the frame.

Another mistake which thousands of players make is to attempt a very delicate shot from a distance of six feet or more, something a professional would not consider even on the few tables which run absolutely perfectly. Time after time, I see novices trickling slowly up to the red hoping to push it just past the green as shown in figure 94, A. Even if the snooker is successfully laid, the escape off the side cushion is easy.

The shot I would play is to push to red in and out of baulk, using some right-hand side to check the cue-ball off the side cushion. Played at the right weight, you could leave a snooker from which your opponent could find it difficult to escape. But even if you don't, it is long odds against him potting the red so you will still be in the game with a chance.

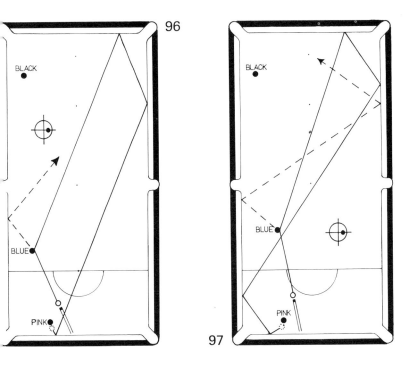

When it comes to leaving snookers, I hardly know where to start because the balls can be positioned in innumerable ways. The best general advice I can give is to develop your knowledge of angles and control of strength as fully as you can, for this will give you the equipment to improvise as the occasion demands. Meanwhile here is a selection for you to practice.

Figure 95 requires a half-ball contact on the brown and some right-hand side so that the cue-ball, just missing the middle pocket, travels off two cushions to finish behind the black. Note here that the position of the blue and pink should help lay your snooker.

Figure 96 requires a particularly fine control of strength and angles. Make the initial thin contact on the blue with right-hand side and bring the cue-ball back behind the pink.

Figure 97 shows a similar shot, but this time using an extra cushion to get the snooker.

Figure 98 is yet another possible way of laying a snooker in this position. Play this time with right-hand side off the left of the blue, using four cushions once more.

Figure 99, a clever snooker behind the black, needs a three-quarter ball contact on the pink, taking the cue-ball with left-hand side off two cushions behind the black.

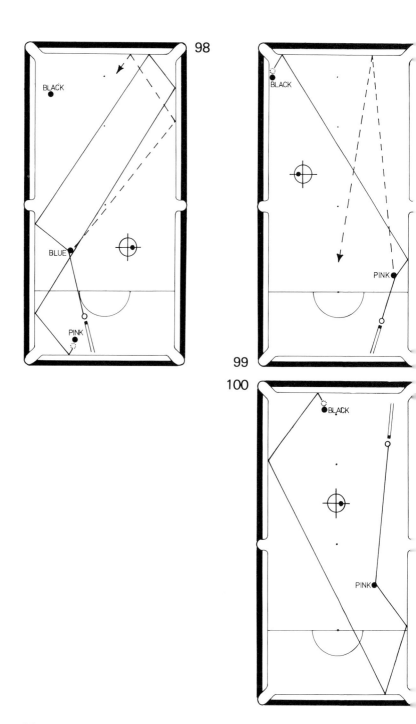

98

98

Figure 100 is a quarter-ball contact on the pink with the cue-ball carrying a little right-hand side to come off four cushions behind the black.

Don't be discouraged if you don't accomplish these shots successfully at once. The angles, strength and amount of side all have to be precisely judged and you will find yourself many times bringing the cue-ball into the general area you require without finding that actual touch to lay the snooker. But if you keep practising, you will gradually develop the feel and confidence which you need on these shots, just as you need them in potting and positional play.

Chapter 10
Escape Play

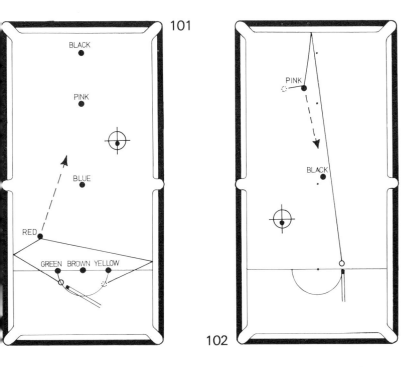

102

The converse of snookering is escaping from snookers, either by using the cushion or by a swerve. As soon as you have gained the most elementary knowledge of angles, some escapes are child's play.

In figure 101, snookered on the last red, you should easily calculate the correct escape route because the red ball is within a few inches of a cushion. When the cue-ball has to rebound more or less straight, as in figure 102, the angle is also easy to calculate. You have, too, the added advantage of having both the ball to hit, the pink, and the spot on the cushion you need to strike with the cue-ball firmly in your line of vision.

Figure 103 shows a much more difficult position. Snookered on the last red your problem is to find the correct angle off the cushion when the object-ball is a long way into the middle of the table. As a generalisation, the cue-ball should leave the cushion (if struck without side) at the same angle it reaches it. However, with wider angles, the cue-ball tends to 'slide' a little, especially when the cloth on the cushions is relatively new. In the 1973 World Championship, an unusually high number of frames were won by players needing snookers, principally because the 'slide' in the new cushions made the escape angles more difficult to calculate than they would have been on tables which had been thoroughly played on.

When you are attempting to escape from snookers like the one in figure 104, when the ball on is in a safe position, it is usually wise to play

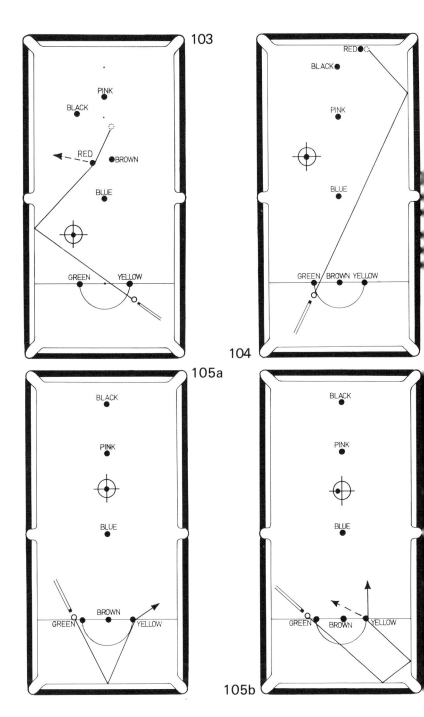

103

104

105a

105b

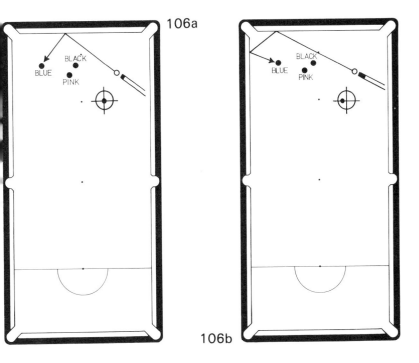

up to it slowly so that whether you just reach it or just fail to reach it, the ball will be safe for your opponent. On the other hand, when the ball on is in the open, give the cue-ball a bit of pace so that, successful escape or not, you put some distance between the cue-ball and object-ball for your opponent.

So far what this chapter has had to say has been pure commonsense but the next stage, an invaluable one in my opinion, is not so obvious. This is what I call the rectangle theory of escaping from snookers.

Given the position in figure 105, most novices would use the one-cushion escape (a), believing it to be easier to calculate than the two-cushion escape (b). This is not so. Not only does 105b enable you to keep the ball you want to hit in vision but the use of a little running side (in this case left) enables you to create a rectangle which, in your mind's eye, is the next best thing to having the escape route chalked on the table.

Figures 106a and 106b show an even clearer illustration of this principle. The escape in 106a is all too easy to miscalculate because there is a long way from the cushion to object-ball and the angle is wide. With 106b, though, the cue-ball is coming off the second cushion at a much straighter angle and the object-ball is near the cushion. Failure to use this escape successfully requires a gross miscalculation.

Figure 107 further demonstrates the principle, and countless other ex-

103

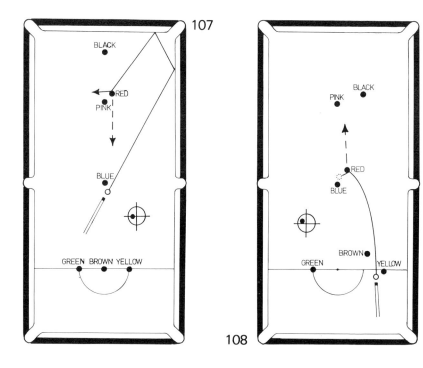

107

108

amples will crop up in game situations. Practise them! I did.

Figure 108, however, shows a situation in which the balls are so awkwardly situated that you cannot use your knowledge of cushion angles and need instead to rely on swerve. This shot is easier with the nap (as shown here) than against it because the nap will help bend the cue-ball back after it has gone round the intervening ball.

Raise the butt of your cue so that you are striking at an angle of about 60°. Aim your cue tip at the left of the cue-ball but, unlike using side normally (where you hit through the ball), strike the cue-ball a sharp glancing blow with the tip moving from centre to left. You may find it a fine distinction between a sharp, glancing blow and a jab but you must feel the tip bite into the cue-ball for the shot to be successful. Keeping the bridge steady—push those fingers into the cloth—and making sure you are striking the cue-ball where you mean to, you should aim the cue-ball well to the right of the brown and then, as the exaggerated side effect comes into operation, see it bend back to hit the red.

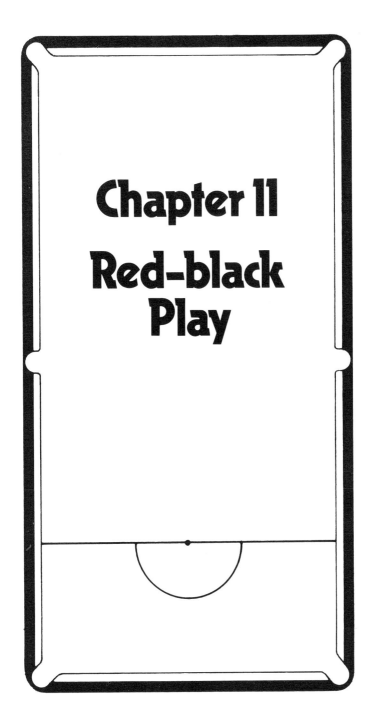

Chapter 11

Red-black
Play

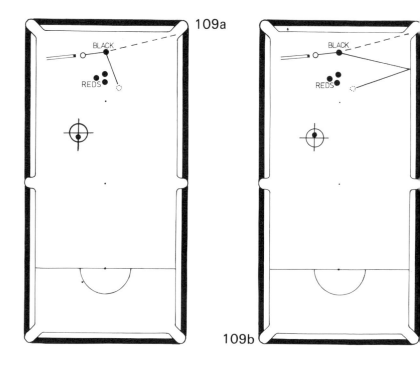

109a

109b

In Chapter 8 I have already touched on red–black play, but because mos
big breaks are compiled round the black spot this is obviously a part of the
game which repays detailed study.

Where a professional's game differs most from an amateur's generally
is in his use of screw and stun where possible in preference to the
cushions. This is particularly evident in my own game, as a comparison
between the six pairs of diagrams shows. The starting position is a
common one, three reds clustered between the pink and black spots. The
'a' diagrams show how ideally I would take the three reds and three
blacks without the cue-ball touching a cushion. The 'b' diagrams show
how the same balls may be taken but using the cushions rather than
screw or stun to gain position. If you compare these two methods, you
will note that the cue-ball travels very much shorter distances in the 'a'
diagrams than the 'b'. This makes your game much more compact, a
quality which pays off when the balls are more awkwardly grouped than
they are here. Speeds of tables and of cushions vary and it is not un-
common to find slow cushions with fast beds and vice versa. This being
so, it is an advantage to be able to eliminate using cushions from your
game as much as possible. On the other hand, there are times when the
position of the other balls may be such that I will employ any or all the
shots in the 'b' diagrams. In short, you must master all the types of shot

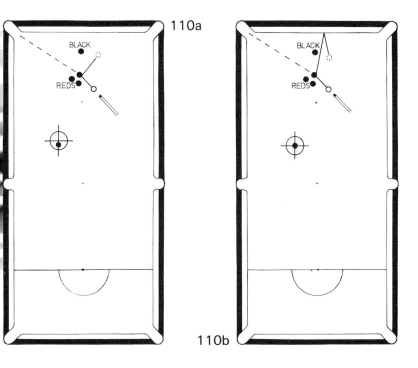

110a

110b

you are likely to meet round the black spot area if you hope to compile big breaks consistently.

In figures 109 a/b, I prefer the sharp stun (a) to the more laborious run through off the cushion (b). Next to playing much too hard and finishing somewhere near the middle pocket, the trap to avoid is leaving yourself so short that, in potting the next red, the cue-ball will cannon into the other two reds. However, if your judgement of strength is good, you should leave yourself nicely above the next red.

The choice in figures 110 a/b is between a soft screw (a) and the bounce off the top cushion (b). Again my preference would be for (a) because spin helps you control the cue-ball to an inch. With the plain ball shot, your control of strength has to have that extra degree of precision, thus requiring extra concentration which is unnecessary with the slow screw.

The general rule in gaining position on the black is: don't leave yourself straight. If you do, the cue-ball can only go straight forward or straight back so you are automatically cutting down the range of shots which are open to you if you leave the cue-ball at an angle to the black.

As you will see, figure 111a is similar to 109a except that the cue-ball is the other side of the black. Again make sure that the cue-ball travels far enough for you to be able to pot the next red (figure 112) without disturb-

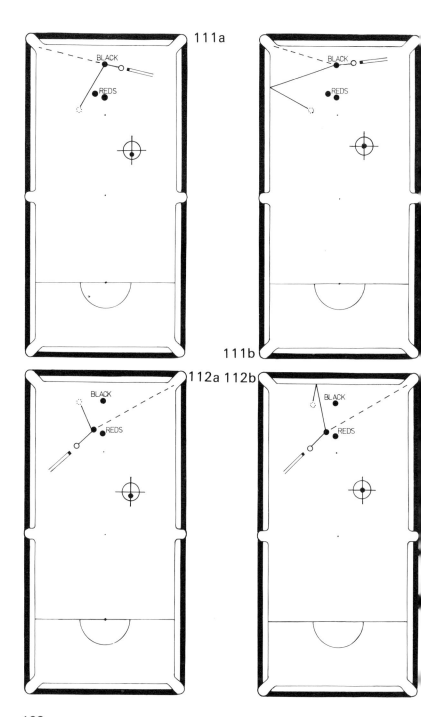

111a

111b

112a 112b

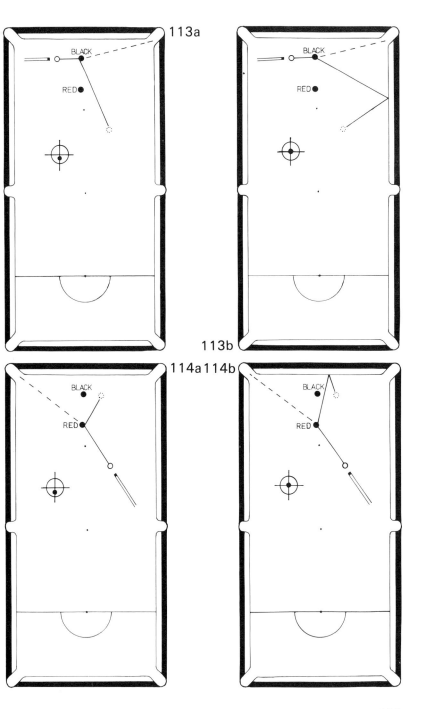

113a

113b

114a 114b

109

ing the remaining red. Figure 111b is, of course, the same shot as 109b

Similarly, in figure 112 the choices are the same as they are in figure 110—the soft screw which I would play (a), or the trickle on and off the cushion (b).

Another point in favour of the screw/stun game over run throughs and using the cushions is the introduction of the new Super Crystalate ball which is lighter and more responsive than the old Crystalate. This has made screw and stun shots easier and run throughs a little more difficult.

Figures 113 and 114 are basically repetitions of earlier shots in the break. With figure 113a, I might consider leaving the cue-ball a little shorter so that I could run through the last red (either direct or off a cushion) in order to leave myself on my preferred side of the table for potting the black and getting on the yellow. If, however, I have to leave the cue-ball as shown in figure 114, I make doubly sure to leave myself a good angle to pot the black. Get straight or almost straight and your chances of getting right on the yellow are virtually nil.

Chapter 12
Splitting the Pack

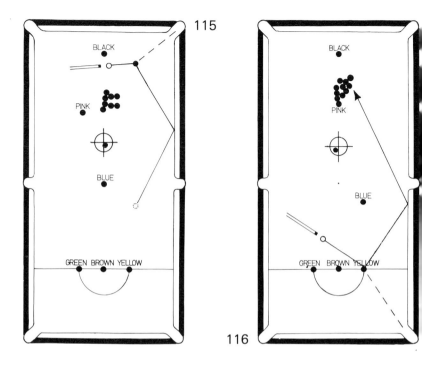

So far, I have discussed situations where the colours are in the open and plenty of reds are pottable, but there are many situations when all the loose reds have been potted and the remaining reds are either in a tight pack and/or under the cushions.

Most amateurs tend to take what is on and, when there is nothing else left, play a safety shot off the pack. This is not my way, nor that of most professionals, for once we have started a break we try everything possible to continue it. Once we settle for ending the break and playing a safety shot off the bunch, there is no telling who will get the next chance. Therefore, when we have taken the open reds, we try to open the pack in such a way that some or all of the remaining reds become pottable.

Many amateurs are afraid to do this because their potting is not sure enough for them not to fear that they will miss the pot and only open the pack for their opponent. This is negative thinking for, provided your positional play has been good enough to leave an easy colour, then the pot should be easy enough for you to devote nearly all your attention to splitting the pack.

The secret of successful pack splitting often lies in your previous shot. In figure 115, for example, many players would, almost without thinking, pot the loose red with a little check side and then attempt the black. This might possibly pay off, but I myself would screw down the table with a little right-hand (running) side to get on the blue. I would only have done

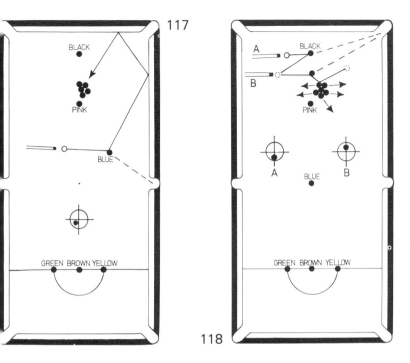

his, however, after noticing the precise lie of the pack, in particular the three reds nearest the pink spot almost in a line across the table.

Get the cue-ball into the middle of these, as shown, and the pack should open with the effect of a stone going into a pond. However, if the original triangular shape of the pack is still recognisable, then I would not attempt to get on the blue if there was a feasible alternative. The reason for this is that the cue-ball will not go into the reds like a stone into a pond but will slide off the side of the triangle like bouncing off the roof of a house and, as often as not, finish in or near the corner pocket.

One point to remember is that a tight pack of 8–10 reds usually requires more force to open it up than a pack of 3–4 reds.

Figure 116 shows a position in which most players would take the blue but this is almost a straight pot, thus making it a very forceful shot to stun into the reds. I would prefer to pot the yellow and take the cue-ball into the pack by screwing off the cushion with left-hand (running) side.

Figure 117 shows another position in which it is possible to screw into the pack. I would play this shot, as shown, with stun and left-hand side.

Whereas, with the direct or one-cushion method, the cue-ball is sometimes slowing down as it reaches the pack, the two-cushion route usually enables the cue-ball to retain its speed. It is also wise to consider, in circumstances when there is more than one route by which the cue-ball can be taken into the pack, which offers the widest target area, cue-

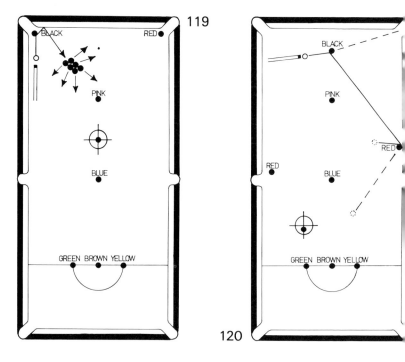

ball's width or two or even three.

It is usual policy to take the loose reds before attempting to open th
pack at the same time as you take a loose red while still leaving positic
on a colour. In figure 118, shot 1 is an easy black but the art is to scre
back to leave an angle on the one remaining loose red so that the cue-ba
can flick off the two back reds to open these out while still leavin
position on the black.

Figures 119 and 120 provide two further examples. In figure 11
many players would trickle in the black (over one top pocket), then trick
in the red over the other top pocket and then possibly attempt to sp
the pack in potting the next black. It is much better, however, to go in
the reds in potting the *first* black. The pack should open nicely even from
medium paced blow and even in the unlikely event of nothing droppir
into an easily pottable position, the original red over the top right-har
pocket is there as an insurance.

In figure 120, there is an easy red over the middle pocket with a
awkward red near the opposite side cushion. In potting the black, it is im
possible not to be in position to pot the easy red, but think boldly in term
of a frame-winning break and try to knock the awkward red out. Th
chances are that you will then take the easy red but with the last red b
now somewhere in the middle of the table you should have little difficul
in potting a colour and getting position on it.

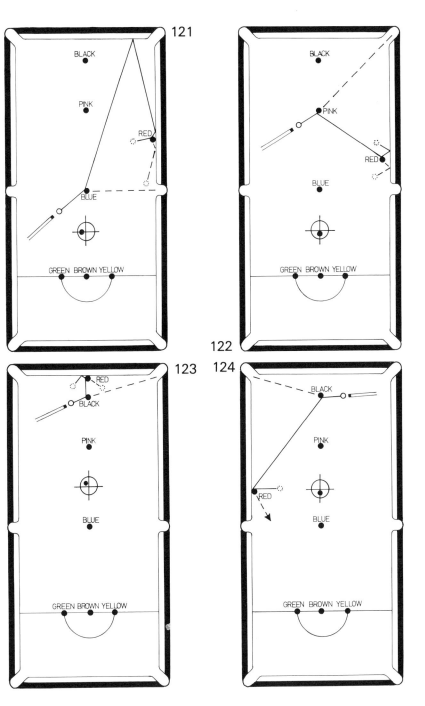

121

122

123 124

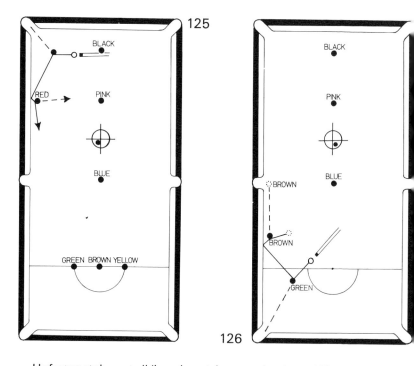

125

126

Unfortunately, not all 'knock-outs' are so simple and I have practised a great deal to develop my touch in this phase of the game.

Figures 121–126 are a selection of 'knock-out' positions which recur often enough to be worth practising. Figure 121 shows how the cue-ball uses the top and side cushions in potting the blue to knock out a troublesome last red. In my experience, the trick lies not in cannoning on to the red but in meeting it at the right strength to nudge it over the pocket.

This also applies to figure 123, though this is a much trickier shot than 122 because the cue-ball, in stunning off the pink towards the red, is going *across* the red rather than coming up behind it.

Variations of figure 123 are constantly cropping up. Often, the secret is to use a little left-hand side to spin the cue-ball off the red.

Figure 124 is a stun from the black to the last red in which there is little margin of error as the red is tight on the cushion.

Figure 125 is much easier because there is room for the cue-ball to get round the back of the red in order to lever it out.

Figure 126 is similar to the last (except that the shot is played in the bottom half of the table). However, the red is slightly nearer the pocket than it is in figure 125 so, even though it is possible for the cue-ball to get round the back of it, I would still prefer to flick it along towards the middle pocket rather than push it out into the middle of the table. I would do this by potting the green with screw and right-hand side.

116

Chapter 13

Plants, Sets and Doubles

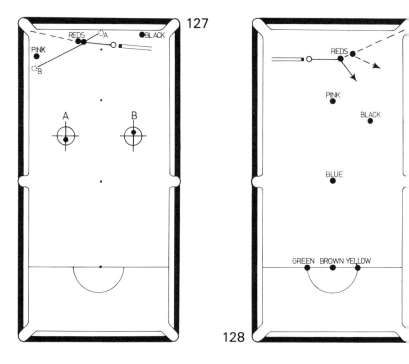

127

128

I have already referred briefly to plants and sets in my chapter on safety
play but it is worth explaining these departments of the game in more
detail since they often hold the key to a frame-winning break.

A set, that is when two reds are touching, is generally easier than a
plant—which is when two reds are not touching. In figure 127, the two
touching reds are so placed that the cue-ball can strike almost any part of
the first red and still pocket the second red. This means that you can, if
you wish, screw the cue-ball straight back, to the left or to the right or
follow through to the left or right for any positional reason you may have.

In figure 128, the reds are not touching so the set becomes a plant
that is, you are not bound to pot the second red unless the cue-ball strikes
the first red at a particular angle. The way to assess this angle is to line up
to pot the second red by using the first red as the cue-ball. Memorise the
spot on the second ball that the first ball needs to strike and then take
your stance behind the cue-ball. Some players find it easier in plant
situations, after cueing up behind the first ball to assess the angle, to
carry the contact point on the second red through to a point on the
cushion.

A plant can not only start or continue a break but can also open up a
pack of reds. In figure 129, the first red in the plant not only sends the
second red into the pocket but, after impact, scatters the reds in the pack
as the cue-ball screws gently for the black.

118

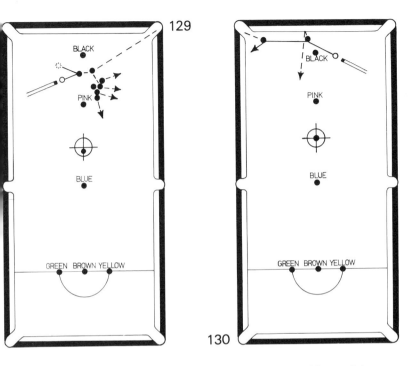

At this point, the pessimists may say that this shot will certainly open the pack—but probably for one's opponent! I would agree to the extent that plants require a very high standard of accuracy and that they can easily go wrong.

Unless the second object-ball is right over a pocket it is rarely a good idea to attempt a plant when there is considerable distance between the two balls. Again, plants are generally easier when you have both object-balls and the pocket right in your sights. With ordinary potting, it is easier to pot into an open rather than a blind pocket and this is even more true where plants are concerned.

Despite these cautionary notes, your confidence and skill with plants will increase the more you practise them. This practice will pay dividends in your safety play since you will notice not only plants which will send an object-ball into a pocket but plants which will send an object-ball not into but over a pocket for your opponent.

Another variety of plant (or combination shot as the American Pool players call them) is shown in figure 130 where the cue-ball strikes two balls, potting the second. Billiards players who are used to playing in-offs have an advantage here as they will recognise the correct angle with the greater certainty.

In figure 130, play off the first red with left-hand side so that as you contact the second red half-ball to send it into the pocket, the cue-ball

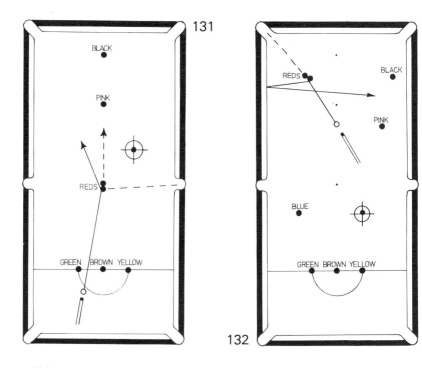

131

132

will bounce off the cushion for the black.

Another 'in-off' shot is shown in figure 131 where there is a red almost touching the blue, apparently a safe position. However, if the cue-ball contacts the red about quarter-ball, it will flick off the blue into the pocket as shown.

Now for the phenomenon which the technically minded may like to puzzle out for themselves: how is it that two touching object-balls which are set so that the second will strike a couple of inches from the pocket (figure 132) can be struck in such a way that the second ball will enter the pocket?

Novices instinctively aim the cue-ball to the left-hand edge of the first object-ball but this will only cause them to miss the shot by an even wider margin. Try instead aiming for the *right*-hand edge of the first object-ball and surprise, surprise . . . some sort of squeeze effect will take place so that the second red enters the pocket.

Doubles

Snooker can sometimes be a relatively simple game when the balls are nicely separated and in the middle of the table, but as we have seen in the chapter on splits and knock-outs, there are many times when the going is much tougher. Indeed, there are times when the break develops in such a way that it is impossible to knock every ball away from a cushion. It is in

120

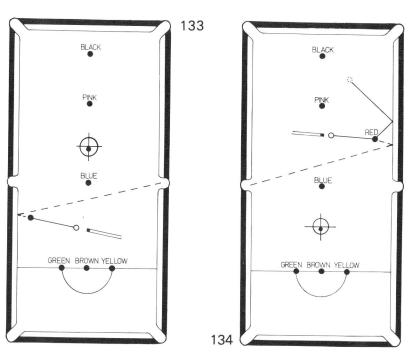

these circumstances that the double really comes into its own.

Except with wide angles, where it tends to slide after it hits a cushion, a ball will leave the cushion at the same angle it strikes it. Thus, in figure 133 you have the most straightforward double of all. With the perfect V shape of the shot it should be said, too, that these are the easiest doubles of all.

Figure 134 is slightly harder because the cue-ball has to strike the object-ball at an angle. Nevertheless, it is still possible to see the object-ball leaving the cushion at the same angle as it strikes it.

When I have object-balls in positions similar to those in figures 133 and 134 I'm not too despondent if I can't knock them out since I would expect to get doubles of this kind nine times out of ten.

The shot in figure 135 is a different proposition as the red is halfway along the cushion. When playing a double of this kind, it seems a little like aiming into space, whereas with the sort of double in figures 133 and 134 there is the guidemark of the middle pocket next to the ball to help you.

Through trial and error, you should soon discover the correct angle to contact the red to double it—which is about as far as novices usually go. However, just as with ordinary pots, you should always pay attention to your positional play. In figure 135 for instance, play strongly enough for the cue-ball to bounce across the table for the black.

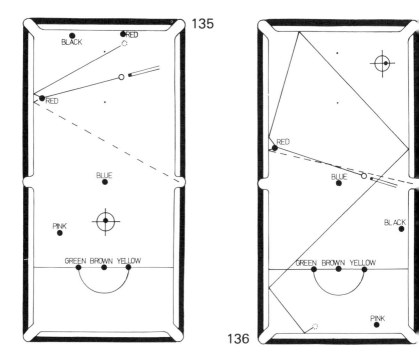

135

136

When you need to use side in a double for positional reasons be very careful as running side tends to widen the angle the *object-ball* takes from the cushion while check side tends to narrow it.

There are many other varieties of double. Figure 136 is a cutback double where some right-hand side is useful to aid the thin contact necessary to slice the ball into the side cushion at the appropriate doubling angle. Figure 137 is a 'cross double' which can often be played, as here, as a shot to nothing. Figure 138 is an unusual top pocket double again played as a shot to nothing and figure 139 is a three-cushion cocked hat double, a shot which has the advantage of cue-ball and black going in opposite directions so that even if the black does not drop, your opponent will still not have an easy shot.

One thing no book can ever give you is experience. There is no substitute for getting on a table and working away at your game. I have discovered far more about the game in solo sessions than I have ever done by playing frames, though there is a place for both in your preparation for what really counts—matches.

The great thing is to enjoy the game. I would rather play Snooker than do anything else and so in a sense I have been able to live for my work rather than work for a living. However tense a match is, I never lose my enjoyment of actually playing. One of the keys to success is to play to the best of one's ability. If you do that, winning will take care of itself.

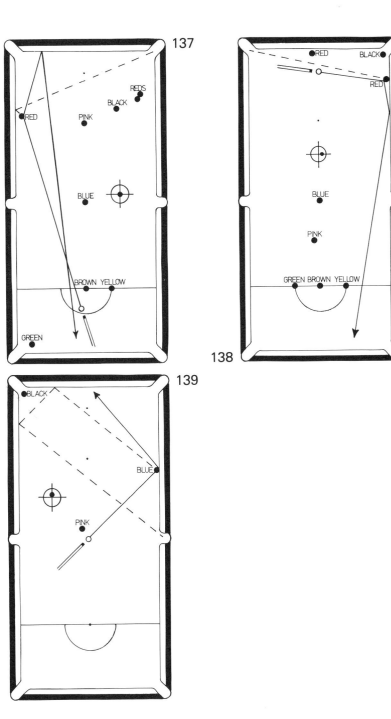

137

138

139

Appendix

Break Analysis 1   142: Pontardulais Conservative Club

My opponent went in-off from the first shot to leave me an obvious slow red in the middle pocket to roll through on to the blue. As figure 140 shows, I chose to play a shot that was far from obvious. Placing the cue-ball as near as possible to the brown for an almost straight pot, I stunned across to take the black in the top pocket. I thought two or three times before I played this but I could see that it wasn't going to be easy to get on the black as it was quite near the pack and wouldn't go in the one top pocket at all. I also thought that if I could pot the black and get it on its spot in the open, a really big break was on.

A little later, a crisis occurred when I attempted to screw from the black into two touching reds but failed to connect and left myself down the table with apparently little chance of continuing the break (figure 141). However, two reds in a cluster of four near the pink spot formed a possible plant although at first glance it appeared that the end red would strike about three inches up the side cushion from the corner pocket. To pot this red, the end but one red had to be struck as near as possible on the extreme right edge. I chose to do this not with the cue-ball (the ultimate position of which would have been unpredictable) but the nearest red. This unusual combination shot opened the cluster of reds and allowed the cue-ball to run off the side and top cushions to finish on the black.

Figure 142 shows the position with four reds left, two touching and not pottable in any pocket and a third on the side cushion. The fourth red was a simple straightforward pot with an obvious black to follow and I chose to screw back slightly to leave a quarter-ball pink. The pink was played sharply with left-hand side so that the cue-ball snicked the cushioned red over the middle pocket and went on to make a cannon on the two touching reds to leave them in the open (figure 143).

After this, the break was relatively plain sailing and I went on to complete a clearance of 15 reds, 12 blacks, 2 blues, 1 pink and all the colours.

Break Analysis 2   147: Broadreeds Holiday Camp

I joined the ranks of the 'maximum men' when I made a break of 147 at

124

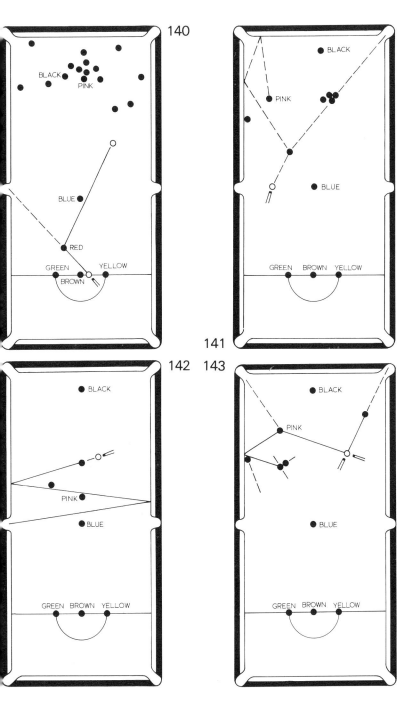

140

141

142 143

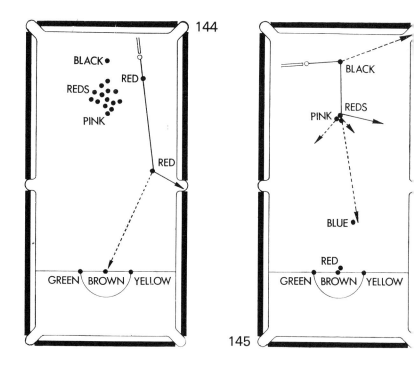

144

145

Pontin's Broadreeds Camp. After my opponent had played a safety sho
there was no red directly pottable but by means of an in-off shot, drivir
one red off another near the middle pocket into the middle pocket,
started the break going (figure 144). The first red finished almo
touching the brown and not pottable in any pocket. This proved cruci
later in the break.

With three reds left, the going looked really sticky as one of these wa
touching by the pink and the other still touching the brown (figure 145

I had obtained a good angle on the black from which to go into the rec
but was afraid that the cue-ball might finish touching or very near the fir
red, especially if I struck it rather full. Therefore, rather than screw a
slow-medium pace into the red, hoping to catch it at an angle, I elected t
strike the cue-ball very little below centre but with more power. When h
hard, the cue-ball takes a wide arc from the object-ball after it has struc
the object-ball at an angle—more of a bounce shot than stun. This left a
easy red into the middle pocket with the cue-ball bounding off th
cushion with strong right-hand side to leave an angle on the black (figur
146).

The second red, however, had come to rest almost touching the blu
so that it was pottable only in the 'yellow' baulk pocket or the opposit
top pocket. I decided to play for it in the baulk pocket because it wa

126

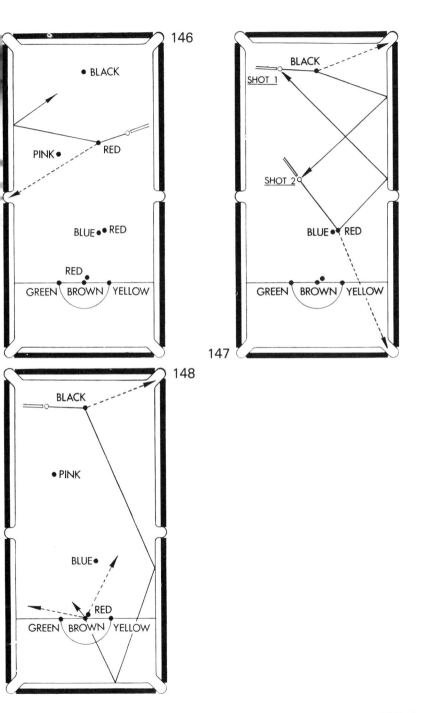

146

147

148

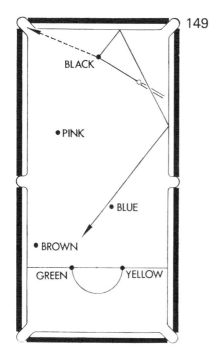

149

easier to get on the black from it than by playing it in the top. If necessary
I could use the blue to help me screw back towards the black but if I had
been potting the red into the top the blue could have got in the way.

The red was potted (figure 147) and the cue-ball taken off the side
cushion to leave a half-ball angle on the black.

I didn't want to leave myself on the black the other side because the
pink was in the way if I used the side and baulk cushions to play a cannon
on the last red and brown. I didn't want to play the cannon off the side
cushion because the cue-ball would have been going towards the baulk
cushion and the red probably towards the side cushion. By using the two
cushions the cue-ball and the red would at least be travelling in more or
less the same direction after contact.

The shot turned out remarkably well. Not only was the cannon itself
achieved—no mean feat—but the red finished at a suitable angle to get
on the black (figure 148). The brown had been kissed near the side
cushion, but I wasn't too worried about that.

However, I dropped in trouble by underhitting the last red and leaving
an awkward angle on the black. I could have played the plain ball shot but
my natural game is a stun game so I decided to use the cushion. I left
myself straight on the yellow as shown in figure 149 from which I left an
angle on the green to cannon on to the brown and clear the table.